THE

OPTOMETRIST'S

GUIDE TO

FINANCIAL

FREEDOM

Drs. Dat Bui and Aaron Neufeld ODs

The Optometrist's Guide to Financial
Freedom

Disclaimer: The content in this book is for informational and educational purposes only and should not be construed as professional financial or tax advice. Should you need such advice, consult with a licensed financial or tax advisor.

For information, please contact:
Email: ODsOnFinance@gmail.com
Website: www.ODsOnFinance.com

Book and Cover design by Aaron Neufeld and Dat Bui ODs

First Edition: November 2019

Table of Contents

The Optometrist's Guide to Financial Freedom

CHAPTER ONE Heavy Gloom: The Reality of Optometry

BY: Aaron

"I can't change the direction of the wind, but I can adjust my sails to always reach my destination."

-Jimmy Dean

So you made your DECISION. You are going to optometry school. You have carefully prepared your applications and aced the OAT (thanks Kaplan). You also have a high GPA from a respectable local university and your letters of recommendation are flawless. In fact, you had a couple extra ones that you couldn't even submit. You volunteered your weekends at a variety of clinics, participated in various university research projects and even went on a weeklong medical mission trip to Haiti. Oh, and that Personal Statement.... You're trying to be humble about it, but it should definitely win a Pulitzer Prize. The only things that stands before you and becoming a doctor are four years of intensive education and a couple board exams.

A DOCTOR.

You'll have a lot of money. A lot more than what you will know what to do with. Life will be easy. It will be all flowers and butterflies.

You'll have a large house with a view and take multiple exotic vacations per year. Fine dining, jewelry, clothes - all included in this deal. At least that is what society will tell you.

Too bad society is **WRONG**

First, you've got that giant looming student loan over your head. That's probably around **$200,000** and maybe even more. What's the interest on that loan? **Close to 7%?** Oh, and you forgot that some of the loans you took out began to accumulate interest while you were in school. Scholarships may help put a small dent in the debt, but it seems increasingly insurmountable as your graduation comes around.

Then, you find a place to settle down and practice. If you find yourself in a highly saturated city after graduation, it is almost certain that you will find employment hard to come by. And the harder the employment is to find, the **lower** your pay will be (damn you supply and demand!). If you are out in the country, you find that patients do not really like to spend money. Or that there just are not that many of them. Different things seem to pile up, contributing to a whittling of income compensation.

Did we mention insurance reimbursement rates? They're at an all time low. Vision insurance companies abuse the profession of optometry on a daily basis. **$40 for an eye exam?** (We're not going to name names).

Was going to school for this long really worth it? The medical model seems a bit promising, but you often find yourself jumping through a variety of hoops. Endless claims rejections, scope of practice and competing ophthalmologists who are perceived to do a "much better job than you do" are just a few of these hoops.

But if that's not enough, just remember there are hundreds of thousands of individuals involved in a variety "disruptive technologies" that are attempting to take you below the knees and reduce your profession to pure automation and mass market convenience. Online eye exams, refraction kiosks, online optical/contact lens suppliers and even full eye examinations done remotely are all being developed.

In fact, five to ten years from when this book is published, they will likely be perfected. So yes, in addition to fellow optometrists, you will also be competing with freaking machines... MACHINES. Supply and demand is most definitely a cruel mistress. Those flowers and butterflies will look a lot like weeds and mosquitos now, won't they?

Wait, It Gets Better...Right?

The purpose of this bleak introduction was NOT to depress you, but rather to give you a reality check. Graduating from Optometry school is only the beginning. The truth is, optometry is not what it used to be. The so-called optometric wishing-well has dried up. **Why?** Well, three main factors are contributing to the ever-shrinking pot available for the eye care industry:

1) Decreasing Reimbursement Rates

Across board, both vision and medical insurances are paying lower and lower amounts for optometric services and materials. What's even worse is that more individuals than ever are under these plans with increasingly low reimbursements

2) Industry Saturation

There are simply more optometrists than there used to be. A finite industry unfortunately and almost automatically translates to less income (on average) to each optometrist. So, why are there more optometrists than ever? Two reasons (1) More schools now exist with larger class sizes. (2) Less optometrists have a solid game plan for retirement, meaning they stay in the workforce longer.

3) Desalination of Industry Capital

Disruptive technologies such as telemedicine, online refraction, subscriptions services and online optical/contact lens shops are all taking from the finite capital of the industry. This is coupled with corporations trying to offer heavily discounted (and oftentimes inferior) services and products. All these desalination factors play into consumer favoritism of **convenience** and **price**, at the cost of **quality**.

Well, that was a depressing list. *Does that mean you cannot be financially successful in optometry?* **Absolutely not.** Many of us in the industry are "killing it" by being financially free and taking home larger incomes that allow for exceptionally comfortable living.

The sad part is that many of our colleagues are not - living paycheck-to-paycheck and being swallowed in debt is usually the norm. This should never be the case.

Herein lies the inspiration for writing this book. Both my co-author Dat and myself have seen plenty of friends and colleagues at both ends of the spectrum. I remember it was around Christmas time, when we sat around a small table in a dive bar one winter evening in 2017, nursing bottled IPAs. We talked about the usual late-20s guy stuff: tough disease cases in clinic, girls they were dating, fast cars; when all of a sudden Dat sprung a question out of the blue:

> *"I wonder how many of our colleagues are prepared for retirement and to be financially free?"*

So the two of us decided to pull out our iPhones and do some research. We asked around and interviewed other optometric colleagues, and even asked other professionals such as dentists, MDs and chiropractors.

The disturbing answer?...... Hardly any of these high-income professionals knew even the basic of the basics about debt, investing or even their own net worth.

The EVEN MORE disturbing news? Many of these individuals were completely inundated with massive debt and did not realize the implications it carried for their futures.

Suddenly, a topic that we seldom talked about in the past became a passion for us. We formed the online discussion group **"ODs on Finance" on Facebook**. The group quickly amassed thousands of members eager to learn and explore the world of finance.

When we started running the group, we were slammed with questions. Our Facebook message inboxes were constantly spitting out with daily new notifications. And through the various discussions we had with colleagues, we were floored by the number of ODs that were living life in debt, some of which were many years further in their lives and careers than us.

So it got us wondering.... How can so many doctors make financially poor decisions and fall into debt? I mean aren't we supposed to be smart?

The answer is SIMPLE. Yes, we are smart. We are smart in our optometric craft. We are smart in diagnosing ocular disease and refracting. However, nothing about finances was ever taught in school. Barring past experience in business/finance or college courses, we basically come out of optometry school being financially inept! This is an unfortunate recipe for disaster for someone going from making NO money to making a sizeable paycheck.

So that's the **GOAL of this book.** To give you a rough guide on how to be financially fit and savvy. In this book, we will lay down a step by step, chapter by chapter guide to becoming not only financially free, but wealthy. In fact, our ultimate goal for any individual reading this book is for that individual to harness and apply the information and skills in this book. If you are reading this book as a student or new graduate, there is absolutely no reason you cannot be debt-free and have a net worth of about $1 million in 5-10 years if you vigorously apply the principles we discuss in this book to your financial discipline, day-in and day-out

Are you riled up? Are you ready to be prosperous? Are you ready to kill it?

We hope you said yes, because we sure are. But before we start our journey, there are few psychological aspects we need to address.
Before attempting to fulfill, it is important to mentally prepare yourself and have the proper mindset.

1) **Lose the Entitlement**
2) **Kill Your Insecurities**
3) **Adopt a Growth Mindset**
4) **Utilize Positive Projection**
5) **Be a Long-Term Thinker**

Building wealth and prosperity does not start when you start practicing as an optometrist. It comes much earlier, even before optometry school. So let's get started and go through these individually.

1) Lose Your Entitlement

Nothing is owed to you when you graduate. In fact, *you owe*, and you probably owe a lot.

One thing that really grinds my gears is the entitlement of a recent graduate (trust me, both authors of this book had the entitlement that we are about to discuss). So many new grads treat their transition from school to work as a big accomplishment. They treat themselves to a gratuitous vacation, a lavish party, a new watch; or maybe all three! They feel that they must metaphorically hold up the Lombardi trophy, when in reality, they have not even made the practice squad!

And it is hard to blame the entitled new grad, especially if they are millennials. Society places a heavy emphasis on giving praise and acclaim to those who graduate as doctors. You're going to get cards, calls and gifts. Everyone would express just how proud they are of you.

But what did you really accomplish? You paid a bunch of money to pass a bunch of classes and exams for four years. You were then given a piece of paper and two letters behind your name in return. This process was done by literally hundreds of thousands of people before you.

So here's the kicker. You really have not accomplished much when you graduate. But you know what the beautiful thing is? *You will accomplish a lot in the future.* Mentally prepare yourself to work even harder than you have ever worked in school.

Unfortunately, entitlement stretches far past graduating. You could be five years into your optometric career and suddenly decide you want an item that is way out of your financial grasp. Your entitlement tells you that you've earned it, but did you really?

Put your passion for your career in full gear. **Be humble** when you start and always look forward. Consistently plan for your future and stop living in the present.

2) Kill Your Insecurities

Part of what leads to entitlement also shares a role in bringing someone to financial ruin. Insecurity.

Insecurity comes in many forms. Material insecurity (I need that new Louis Vuitton bag!). Emotional insecurity (Oh, they are always talking behind my back!). Physical insecurity (My body does not look like hers!). More pertinent to the theme of this book are material and physical insecurity. It is easy to get caught up, trying to keep up with

Joneses or trying to match that Instagram influencer (and trust me, that Ferrari in the photo is a rental!).

Develop a solid version of you. **You are Awesome.** You are an amazing practitioner who is going to help many patients. Through your work, you will become wealthy both in money and in spirit.

The most important part of killing your insecurities is being self-aware. Know yourself and your pitfalls. You will never be able to completely eliminate your insecurities, but if you know what they are, you are less likely to become a victim to them.

3) Adopt a Growth Mindset

Before we approach the actual framework of building wealth, we first must align our mindset with our goals. In her award-winning book *Mindset*, Carol Dwecker defines two types of mindsets: the fixed mindset and the growth mindset. The fixed mindset presents a complacent mind. It believes that it has learned all that it needs to learn. It avoids anything that might result in failure, because it believes it is too good to fail. It finds learning new things and being out of its comfort zone, unappealing and even offensive.

On the contrary, the growth mindset is a mind that is constantly seeking out challenges. It is not afraid to fail, because it realizes that failure is often the greatest teacher. It approaches every situation as an active learner, rather than a complacent expert.

To achieve financial freedom and be the best doctor you can be, apply the growth mindset to everything you do. In no way, will the journey be easy. It will present constant challenges, but the rewards will be more than worth it.

4) Utilize Positive Projection

Positive projection (first coined as one of the 10 keys of closing a sale in the book *Secrets of Closing the Sale*: by Zig Ziglar) is the concept of visualizing success or victory in a challenge before attempting a challenge and then maintaining this visualization throughout the attempt at the challenge. In essence, you enter a challenge after you have already tasted the victory mentally.

Your journey out of the abyss of debt and into the throws of wealth will be riddled with pitfalls and dejection. You'll see pictures of friends at a music festival while you slave away on a Saturday working. Your son or daughter will ask you why they cannot have a backyard pool like the neighbors. Your colleagues will wonder why you do not want to dine with them at the local Michelin star restaurant.

It is important to keep your goals at the forefront of your mind. A nice dinner will give you a few hours of fun; eliminating debt and having piece of mind financially can last a lifetime.

5) Be a Long Term Thinker

When one builds wealth, a long-term vision must constantly be envisioned. Shortsighted thinking (no pun intended) can be deadly to your long-term financial security. Silly luxuries and temporary things often appear more appealing than your 401K, IRA and student loan repayment. To be blunt, having the patience to pursue long-term financial goals can be brutal and not fun. Lavish living crosses every budding optometrists mind every once in a while. But just how financially damning can short term thinking hurt you?

Let's explore the Doctor Car Story.

Dr. Awesome and Dr. Basic just graduate from optometry school with $250,000 in debt (7% interest) and both land jobs that pay $120,000 a year. Let's assume they have roughly equal living expenses. Dr. Basic embodies short-term thinking and Dr. Awesome embodies long-term thinking.

Dr. Basic immediately purchases a brand new BMW 3 series, because he now is a doctor and thus needs a "Doctor Car". MSRP comes out to

$50,000. Of course he just graduated, so he will have to make payments. He gets a favorable APR of 5% on 5 years of financing.

Dr. Awesome on the other hand decides to continue driving her Honda Civic beater. She applies the money she would have spent for the car on her student loans.

Let's explore Dr. Basic's long-term debt from his decision to be "cool." He will have to pay roughly $1500 per month for the car, not to mention increased insurance premiums, maintenance costs, and premium gasoline (add another $250 per month, give or take). That $1500 that could have been applied to his student loan debt will continue to accrue interest.

So how does this affect Dr. Basic over the period of loan repayment? Running the numbers through the accounting program *T-Value* shows that Dr. Awesome's total loan repayment amount after aggressively paying off her loan is **$267,159.90.**

What about Dr. Basic's total repayment amount? **$325,566.50.** If we take the difference between their grand totals $58,406.60 + $65,000 (car price + necessary attached expenses), the car actually cost a **_whopping $123,406.60!_** That's a steep cost for a little bit of social insecurity.

When approaching financial thinking and financial security, it's important to look at the long term. Money saved now, can be far more valuable than money saved later if it is invested properly. Frivolous items may appear desirable, but a life where finances are planned out and debt is never an issue is far more fulfilling and comfortable. Your long-term approach to your finances can never occur too soon.

In fact, it should begin to happen even before you start your journey to becoming an optometrist.

The 10 Commandments for the Financially Secure Optometrist

1) Pay off your debts as quickly as possible
2) Invest early and often
3) Live way below your means
4) Maintain a budget
5) Insure yourself heavily against severe catastrophes
6) Take advantage of all tax breaks
7) Strive to own your home when you have the right finances
8) Don't leverage too much and value yourself professionally
9) Own your career and if you can swallow it, your own practice
10) Seek unbiased, well-educated advice

The Optometrist's Guide to Financial Freedom

CHAPTER TWO: How Does Money Work? BY: Aaron

"You try to give me your money. You better save it, babe. Save it for you rainy day."

-Jimi Hendrix, "Fire"

Money is one of the biggest topics in the world. It is constantly debated. It is attributed as the catalyst to some of the greatest successes and is also blamed as the reason for some of the biggest failures. The truth is, money makes the world run. Without money and the governmental structures that enforce its continuous use, we would be nothing but a lawless society finding sustenance and survival in the hunter/gatherer gamesmanship of our ancestors. The fact that money is so polarizing in both its effects on humans and the effects that it experiences on behalf of its human handlers means one thing: money is a fickle beast.

An individual's relationship to money can be defined in two ways: Someone who is a money loser and someone who is a money gainer. A **Money Loser** is someone who essentially pisses money away, someone that loses more money than he or she can accumulate - throwing earned money at depreciable assets at a rate in which recuperation is impossible often does this. A **Money Gainer** is someone who builds stores of money, often through the utilization of appreciable assets (or investments).

Now here is the kicker. Anyone can be a money loser. The good news is that anyone can be a money gainer. Take for instance the NBA star point guard that signs a contract for $10 million a year. He plays for 10 years, and in that time, he owns multiple cars, jets, mansions and throws elaborate parties.

Yet, five years out of retirement he finds himself bankrupt like 60% of his NBA peers.[1] This washed-up hoops phenomenon is a money loser, his net worth is just as much as the homeless dude sitting on the corner of the street begging for change.

Now consider your friendly neighborhood landscaper. Through 12-hour days of hard labor, 6-7 days a week, he grosses about $50,000 a year. He places half of his earnings in investment vehicles and spends frugally. After 20 years of brutal work, Mr. Landscaper retires a millionaire and travels the world (while Mr. NBA star attempts to find a job bussing tables at IHOP). Our friendly neighborhood landscaper is a money gainer, and comes out as the winner in this story.

Now the point of this illustration is to show you that literally anyone can be a money loser, whether they are of a high-income class or not.

Consider this harrowing statistic: **78% of the US workforce work from paycheck to paycheck.** That is absolutely insane. That's doing a trampoline routine with no safety net. That's an Evil Knievel jump without a helmet (or any motorcycle experience for goodness sake!). But consider the flipside, nearly anyone can be a money gainer as well.

The goal we have for you after finishing this book is for you to have the necessary understanding of money in order to achieve financial freedom. *We want you to be a money gainer.* But before we dive into the specifics on mutual funds, real estate investing and insurance, let's first understand how money can work for us and subsequently against us.

---

[1] According to a 2008 article in *The Star* about NBA players' financial security - our guess is that this statistic is probably higher today.

The key to understanding our fickle friend, Mr. Money and how to make him expand and grow lies in three vitally important concepts:

1) Income and Expenses (I/E)
2) Assets and Liabilities (A/L)
3) The IEAL Machine + IEAL Synergy

INCOME AND EXPENSES

If you break the word income apart you find a simple compound word composed of "in" and "come." This makes sense, income described money that is "coming in" to you. Most refer to **income** as their take home pay. Whether it is from the check they receive every two weeks from being employed at the local VA or from the monthly distribution they take out of their private practice. While it is common to think of this direct income as the only source of income, there are actually three types of income.

- **Earned Income**
- **Portfolio Income**
- **Passive Income**

Earned income or direct income is what we mentioned in the previous paragraph. It is the money you make from your day job, whether it is hourly pay or salary. Earned income is the most instantaneous of the incomes and is thought by many to be the most reliable of the incomes. However, due to these factors, earned income is also the most taxed income, both due to its consistency and prevalence.

Portfolio income revolves around income made from investing in stocks, bonds, mutual funds, etc. It comprises your 401K, IRA and any taxable accounts you may have through entities such as Vanguard, Fidelity, etc. Portfolio income tends to be cyclical and can be volatile as it is dependent on factors beyond an individual's control. The key term that differentiates Portfolio income from Earned and Passive Income is consistency.

Passive income involves consistent income that comes to you via investment vehicles that are within your control. For most individuals this will be rent collected on real estate investments. For other individuals this may include royalty payments, payments on patents, or autonomous business entities. Note that your private practice income falls under earned income, unless you have found a way to completely remove yourself from your practice but still collect the dough -- if this is the case, then you should immediately put down this book and write one yourself, because you have a New York Time Bestseller on your hands.

And now for the less sexy part. The term **Expenses** encompasses anything that takes away from your income. This includes items purchased, food, rent, taxes, student debt payment, mortgage and nearly everything else under the sun that costs money and is either necessary or unnecessary for living.

Pitting your income against your expenses shows your ***Instantaneous Financial Health.*** Think of it as a snapshot in the here and now. Income numbers are given a positive number and expenses are given a negative number.

If your overall health is in the red/negative - you need help! This is not a sustainable lifestyle and will lead you to ruin. To get out of the red/negative and into the black/positive you either increase the Income column (tough) or decrease the Expenses column (easy). We will have a much more in-depth look at this in our Budgeting chapter. Right now, we are still just understanding how money works.

Take a look at the **Instantaneous Financial Health Analyzer,** aka Income/Expense Chart, below. Are you in good financial health?

Income[2]	Expenses
-Paycheck (earned income) -Passive Income	-Food -Clothing -Misc. Items -Credit card monthly payment amount -Student loan monthly payment amount -Car monthly payment amount -Mortgage or rent monthly payment amount -Taxes -Real Estate taxes (if applicable) -Insurance premiums - health, renters/homeowner, etc.

ASSETS AND LIABILITIES

Ok, now that we have a more solid grasp on income and expenses, let's talk about assets and liabilities. You've definitely heard the terms 'assets' and 'liabilities' at some point in life. While these terms are vital for judging business performance and profitability, they can have a more basic application to personal finance.

Assets simply represent things that *give you value*. This includes your house, your personal belongings and your retirement portfolio. Quite simply, assets are things that make you worth money. These include any real estate holding, your portfolio holdings (stocks, bonds, mutual funds, etc), and any liquid cash you are holding.

Liabilities on the other hand, are the antithesis of assets and incorporate things that *take value away*. Liabilities include student debt, credit card debt, car payments, and mortgages.

---

[2] Note that Portfolio Income is not included because it is 1) not a liquid asset (not useable right away) and 2) is often stored with a target disbursement date

When assets and liabilities are pitted against each other on a piece of paper, this is deemed a **Balance Sheet**.

Assets	Liabilities
-Real Estate	-Mortgage
-Retirement Portfolio	-Student loan debt
-Cash in Savings/Checking Account	-Credit card debt
	-Car loan debt

Once again, we can assign positive values to asset and negative values to liabilities. The difference represents your <u>overall financial health</u>, better known as your **Net Worth**.

So, while income and expenses give you a value of your financial health at a current point in time, assets and liabilities give you a better idea of your financial health over time through net worth. To use an analogy familiar to a doctor, think of a diabetic patient:

1) **Income/Expenses** = represent Blood Sugar
2) **Assets/Liabilities/Net worth** = represent A1C count (if this isn't ringing a bell, pick up your physiology textbook and get some remedial studying in!).

Income/Expenses and Assets/Liabilities Synergy

Ok, so at this point you're probably thinking "Well now, I understand how asset, liabilities, income and expenses relate to me; but this hack told me he would get my net worth to seven digits...So what gives?"

Relax a bit and take a step back.

Now that we have our basic concepts, let's see how we can relate them to real world transactions. Let's explore how these four terms work synergistically either very much for you OR very much against you.

Much like when you learned to treat glaucoma, you first needed to learn

1) The different parts of the eye, followed by
2) The physiology of the eye and its relation to the optic nerve
3) Methods of treating glaucoma.

Our definitions above represent the anatomy, now let's jump into the physiology and explore the synergy of these concepts. Once we understand the synergy, we can then understand how to manipulate this synergy, to our favor.

First, let's burn this image into our brains:

This will be our diagram of our four concepts working together. This four-headed synergistic beast, which we will now lovingly refer to as the **IEAL Machine** (because we want to be super original here - does sarcasm convey well over text?) can be found working in two different environments:

- **Self vs. Debt Collector**
- **Self vs. Debtor**

All right, let's go a little deeper.

Self vs. Debt Collector

Let's say you just got your very first paycheck as an employed optometrist (Go you!). You are feeling awesome and decide to take all your friends out for drinks. You buy everyone a few rounds, because, hey, you're freaking awesome and liquid courage is really speaking to you. The total bill is $500 when everyone decides to leave the bar.

Let's send this through the IEAL machine.

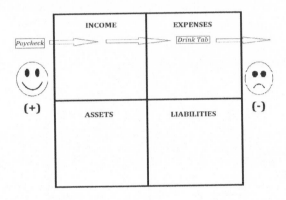

Pretty simple. Money goes into your account, you purchase a product (in this case 45 shots of Patron...or 92 pints of Coors Light), and money goes out of your account.

Let's say you decide to *use a credit card to make your purchase*, rather than cash that was assumed in the previous schematic. Let's run the IEAL machine again:

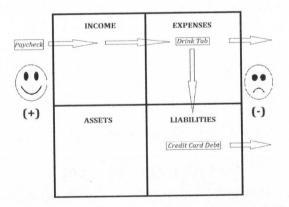

Now we can see that instead of an immediate expense, the credit card debt incurred by the purchase now *turns it into a liability*. Keep in mind that the expense still exists, because you will have to pay for the expense at some time in the future. The difference now is that that expense could possibly be more if you let your credit card debt sit and let interest pile on it.

Obviously, placing a large bar tab on your credit card affects both your financial health and net worth in a negative way. Remember: income/expenses relate to immediate financial health and assets/liabilities relate to net worth.

But much like the First Law of Thermodynamics that states that energy cannot be created or destroyed in a closed system, so too does the same principle apply to money in a transaction. So, who benefits from your incurred alcohol debt?

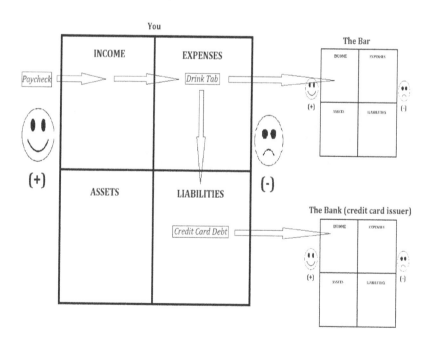

Hope you're not having flashbacks from ray tracing exams in 1st year Optics class! But as you can see, your hard-spent money goes to two debt collectors, the bar and the bank. What you see right above you is the *cycle of consumerism.* This is the reason that as businesses flourish, people are employed and housing/stock prices go up. Why?

Because if we expanded these schematic further, we would see that under "The Bar's" and "The Bank's" Expenses component there would be Employee Payroll (Mind blown? You're welcome).

This cycle of consumerism is also how most people view the only way to use money. Sadly, it is the reason 78% of America lives paycheck to paycheck. They cannot get out of the cycle of consumerism. They hemorrhage money at a rate in which it is impossible to keep more than they spend.

The 78% is like a collective hamster stuck running in a spinning wheel that goes nowhere.

Well, you don't have to be that hamster. It's time to break out of that cage and run free. But how? The solution is brutally simple. Reverse the cycle.

Self vs. Debtor

That's right. Instead of owing the debts, be the one that issues the debts. Sure, throughout life you will always have debts in the form of expenses and liabilities. But if you can get your money to work for you, you can turn back the cycle in a way where your income and assets continually rise, while your expenses and liabilities continually fall. This is called *achieving financial freedom.* Or as they call it in the streets, being rich.

The process cannot happen overnight. In fact, it takes a lot of time and even more patience. Assets such as stock/bond holdings, businesses you own, and real estate investments can help tip the cycle heavily in reverse, and subsequently, heavy in your favor.

Say for instance, you buy some real estate: a two-bedroom condo that you rent out to a nice couple. Let's compare their IEAL machine to your IEAL machine:

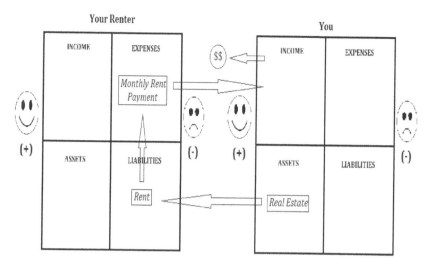

Look at how much better that is than our previous example of grabbing watered-down tequila in a dive bar! You could run a similar model if you own a practice or other business entity. *Just replace "monthly rent payment" with "materials" or "services."*

What this chapter serves as is a primer for your approach to money. When you get your paycheck, think of that money as something that can grow and create more money with. Think of the IEAL machine whenever you get tempted by a large purchase (or even a small purchase). Most unneeded material items (for example, jewelry, clothes, etc.) and fleeting purchases (for example, lavish and unneeded vacations) are sunk costs that increase not only your expenses, but also your liabilities.

Always find ways to fill the Assets component of your IEAL machine. You will continually generate income and set yourself on a course for financial freedom.

Throughout this book, we will go into many specific methods of eliminating liabilities (debt and expenses) and building assets (retirement funds, property, etc.).

It's time to access your blueprint for financial success.

The Optometrist's Guide to Financial Freedom

CHAPTER THREE: The Best Investment You Can Make in School is You BY: Aaron

"Believing and investing in yourself is the best way to shift your thinking from a paradigm of excuses to one of solutions."

— Farshad Asl

The moment you finish undergraduate studies and choose to go to Optometry school, you are incurring a completely different financial situation than your undergrad peers who immediately enter the workforce. So what is the first step in beginning your financial journey as an optometrist? *Start school immediately.*

Gap Year Blues

Many individuals will tell you that a gap year or two between college and post-graduate studies is helpful and relevant. In my opinion (and many others), this simply is a waste of time and precious resources. If you are certain you want to go optometry school and become a doctor, apply during your last year of undergrad. Apply to as many schools as you think necessary based on the competitiveness of your application, then apply to a few more. You can always turn down interviews if needed.

Taking a year off should only be considered if you need more time to consider whether you want to enter the profession. Using a gap year to work as a technician, obtain a Master's degree (I am talking to all you Public Health Master/OD out there who just haved More Debt), or do volunteer work to "boost" your application simply do not make sense when you consider those years are potentially loss in six figure income years.

The final argument for a gap year is to *prevent burnout.* The unfortunate mistake behind this mentality is that you will be working at least 20 to 30 years after you graduate optometry school. By the time you finish college, you are already well into adulthood. It is time to hunker down and take the reigns. *Time to grow up and be an adult.* The idea of having a break before doing work should be a thought of the past.

The 2x Rule

In optometry school, you have two options when paying for tuition, your rent, your food or even a squishy toy for your dog:

1) You pay for it with money you currently have
2) You pay for it with money that is loaned to you

Obviously, option A is clearly your best choice in any sort of purchase. However, being a student will most likely push you to utilize option B to fund your education and living situation. *This is fine* - in many cases there is really no way around this - but approach it with a consistent caution.

Enter the 2x Rule. *The rule is simple.* Whenever you purchase anything with loan money, multiply the price by 2x and assume that is the price you are incurring. Extra piece of equipment for $200, think of it as $400 in ***future dollars.*** New pair of jeans for $50, think of it as $100. Using this mentality will help keep you honest, and keep you from making rash and frivolous choices.

Will these purchases really cost you 2x in the future when you pay off your loans? *Yes or no.* They may cost less if you pay off your loans quickly or may be more than double if you pay off your loans at a slower pace! Ingrain this methodology (or one similar to it) into your thought process as you read through the rest of this chapter and as you go through school.

Choosing Your School

When approaching the optometry school application from a purely financial perspective, there are three factors that can play a huge role on the money you will be left owing from your four-year experience (keep in mind that finances should not be your number one priority when choosing a school, but they should be factored into the equation).

> 1) Tuition Rate
> 2) Location
> 3) Quality of School

1) Tuition Rate

When we think cost of education, tuition is obviously the first thing that comes to mind. When selecting an optometry school to attend be mindful of tuition rates. Obviously, choose the school with the lowest tuition rate that fits your needs. If possible, find a history of tuition rate changes for your schools of interest as well, since schools have the right to raise tuition every year.

Another aspect to keep in mind is in-state vs. out-of-state tuition. In-state tuition rates, if offered, tend to be substantially less that out-of-state tuition rates. Additionally, certain schools allow you to claim in-state tuition rates after you have lived in the state for a year.

2) Location

The location of your school will play a huge factor in your cash flow and your student loan debt. Rents can widely vary based on where you end up for your optometric education. The authors of this book

(Dat and myself) can provide a telling example of location disparity during our time in school from 2011-2015:

Author	Aaron	Dat
School	Southern College of Optometry	Southern California College of Optometry
Location of Living	Inner city Memphis	Los Angeles
Rent	$500/month	$900/month

But it does not just stop at rent. General living expenses can vary drastically based on geographic location. Even the recreational activities you choose to partake in relative to the region where your school lies in will add up over time. If you spend your weekends camping in the Missouri woods, you will probably incur substantially less expenses than exploring nightlife in Los Angeles City.

When thinking about location, also consider the location of your living quarters. In certain areas, staying closer to school may substantially raise your cost of living, and thus commuting in may be wiser. However, in other areas, rents may be similar, and it would be wise to save some gas money.

Your fourth year of optometry school can have a huge or miniscule impact on your total debt upon graduation. In your fourth year (unless if you choose to stay local), you will most likely be moving around for rotations. One of my biggest regrets was not planning far ahead for rotations. I landed a fantastic rotation in La Jolla, CA, but ended up saddled with a small apartment that was renting for $1700/ month! The rent for that semester ended up being roughly equal to a whole year's rent in Memphis. Be smart and plan out affordable housing for your rotations, especially since each of them will only be for a few months.

3) Quality of School

This section may be a bit controversial, and to some, maybe a bit offensive. However, remember that we are approaching this from a purely financial cost/benefit perspective - the quality of your optometry school matters.

All optometry schools are created equal, right?

An eternal optimist may say so, and sure, all optometry schools are accredited. However, it is important to take a look at the numbers. When considering schools, look at different factors such as focus on specialties, quality of educators, practice philosophies and board passage rates. All these factors will not only affect you financially, but also professionally. Each and every optometry school provides a unique mix of factors that may appeal to one individual but not to the other. Every person is different, and thus your needs to lead you down a road to success will be different as well.

We hold a firm belief that the passage rates for National Boards provides a higher reflection on quality of school and the education that is provided, rather than individual performance of the students. That being said, we are not discouraging you from attending any particular optometry school, however keep it in mind how the quality of your school can affect your transition into being a practicing optometrist.

How to Pay For School?

Now for (arguably) the most important part of this chapter. *How do I pay for my schooling?*

Well, the answer is simple. **Pay for as much of your schooling as possible up front, and then take out loans for the rest**. If you have money in the bank, or if your parents have money and they are willing to gift you; use it all towards your optometric education. Keeping extra money in the bank (or buried in the backyard) during optometry school is a huge financial mistake.

> **Student loans have a guaranteed
> return. All other investments do NOT.**

Compounding interest from student loan debt will always win out over high yield savings accounts, CDs, bonds, or even mutual funds. This is because the interest rate on your loan is consistent and will follow you to your grave. Investments such as stocks, mutual funds and real estate may have an upside, but they carry risk and no guarantee of a positive return. High yield savings accounts and CDs allow for some interest accrual, but they will not be anywhere near the level of your student loan interest. Use any disposable income towards lowering the initial principal debt you will incur.

Limiting Your Accumulating Debt while in School

You can accumulate a mirage of expensive debt that will only continue to increase while you are in school. Without a source of steady income plus the addition of living expenses and a large tuition bill, your net worth can nosedive into the red rather quickly. The following five financial pointers will help keep your debt in check once in school:[i]

1. **Obtain Scholarships**
2. **Limit Loans**
3. **Limit Equipment Purchases**
4. **Work Part Time**
5. **Live like a Poor Student**

1) Obtain Scholarships

The greatest thing about higher education is that your future peers as well as society want you to succeed. Heck, even the government and banks want you to succeed. But why all the positivity? Because inevitably, it all comes back around. Entities that invest in your personal success will benefit either monetarily, physically or emotionally. When you have a driving force behind your future career, it means that plenty of incentives will be available. This means that if you try your darnedest and are recognized for your efforts, you will have leverage, specifically in the form of scholarships.

Scholarships come in all shapes and sizes. Many require applications or essays. Some are based on merit, while others may simply be based on ethnicity or demographic. Some scholarships are based on location and may require you to serve time in that location after graduation. These can be quite lucrative, but remember to have your heart set on practicing on the specific location before accepting.

Apply for as many scholarships as you can. Even if the scholarship is for a small amount of money or a piece of optometric equipment, it can still help. Leave no stone unturned!

Military scholarships present an interesting conundrum. On the plus side, obtaining a military scholarship covers your schooling costs and allows you to serve your country, entering at the rank of Captain. A military scholarship enables you to graduate optometry school (relatively) debt free. On the negative side, a military scholarship normally requires a three-year commitment as a military optometrist post-graduation. Your income level will be heavily dwarfed (annual salary was around $60,000 when I was in school) while you serve for three years. Finally, you could be shipped to an area of service that you did not necessarily want to be in.

Our advice is that if you want to obtain a military scholarship, do not do it just for the covered tuition. Make sure your heart is set to serve the United States and have an open mindset towards possibly landing somewhere you did not necessarily want to live.

3) Limit Student Loans

I remember going to a party in my first year of optometry school (yes, I actually remembered). Before heading over, a buddy and I headed to the local liquor store to pick up a "contribution." My buddy picked up an extra-large bottle of Grey Goose that came to a grand total of $60.

When he was paying for it, he said something with a smile that made my gut hurt: "It's ok, the loans are paying for it."

Utilizing and abusing loan money is easy. In fact, it's too easy, and with good reason. The more money you take out in loans, the more money Sallie Mae makes off of you! That money sure as hell is not free, but it sure feels free. All in all, the access to funds can be alluring, so place a mental block on taking out additional funds. Think of loan money as poison or fire, something that you do not want to handle.

In Chapter 1, we talked about how a luxury car purchase right out of school can significantly impact you financial. Now think of that pricey bottle of vodka. That purchase occurred four years before my buddy (who happens to be a wonderful optometrist) even generated a positive income. If you truly do the math, the bottle's long-term cost was probably a full day of work.

3) Limit Equipment Purchases

Optometry school sets itself apart from other professional schools in one distinct area. Equipment purchase. Who realized that such a small part of the body would require so many large, innovative, and extremely expensive pieces of equipment. On average, you will accumulate roughly **$15,000 worth of equipment** in optometry school. This is a huge expense, and unless you are planning to make a career as a traveling optometrist or start up a private practice; you probably won't use that equipment and may end up selling it after school (for a reduced price).

When you are in school, you will be tempted to buy everything and anything. This feeling makes complete sense. You are learning your craft and becoming more efficient so you want the best tools to do so. Try to be a minimalist with your equipment purchases. Only buy equipment you need and try to buy used. Avoid extra equipment (keep the Panoptic on the shelf for now) and stick to the basics. A 90D lens has worked for decades and will work just fine for you. The newest

Volk lens are simply marketed to grab a few extra Benjamin's out of your wallet.

Some schools, including mine, will mandate that you buy your equipment at the start of semester or year. The equipment will be brand new and prices will reflect this. If you can, try returning and buying used, or if possible, even consider renting equipment.

4) Work Part Time

Working part time is a fantastic way to at least partially alleviate the inevitable student loan headache you will face post-graduation. There are many low stress, part time jobs you can take on in optometry school including work-study programs offered by your college. Working as a tech or optician can give you valuable experience and possibly help plant your foot in the door for a starting job out of optometry school. Our best advice is to choose a job that allows you to multitask studying and working. Librarian or proctor positions are great for giving you a little income while still allowing study time.

A word to the wise for your optometry school years: ***DO NOT work too hard at your side job!***

Remember that you are primarily at school to learn, not to make money (and not to party all the time). If your grades start to suffer or if you begin feeling burnt out, it is time to cut down your working hours or possibly stop all together. Remember that your part time income while at school is no comparison to what you will make once you are out of school. Do not compromise your future if you cannot find a work/study balance.

5) Live Poor and Set up a Monthly Budget

Chances are, you have heard the phrases "live like a student" or "live like a doctor." "Live like a student" implies living poorly or basically just using the bare necessities to get by. "Live like a doctor" implies a more lavish lifestyle, ripe with, well, wastefulness.

The Optometrist's Guide to Financial Freedom

When you are in school, you are constantly undergoing negative cash flow. Every minute you spend in lecture, lab or even the school restroom is a dollar being lifted out of your pocket and accruing interest.

So how do you ensure you don't dig yourself into a deeper money pit while in school? Set up a budget! (Don't worry; we will go more into depth in later chapters on how properly set a budget)

If you really try, your living expenses while in school can be under $500 a month. If that seems tough, there is absolutely no reason they should exceed $1000 (rent excluded in these cases).

Planning for financial success while you are still in the student position is tough. Up until this point, you most likely have not had to deal with money at the level of someone that is working a full-time job. This means your perspective is a bit different. Temptation abounds in school, especially when friends and colleagues participate in lavish activities. The key is to keep the long term in mind.

Planning for long-term wealth starts early. Draw up a budget and stick with it, you are on your way to success!

CHAPTER FOUR: How to Tackle your Massive Student Debt? BY: Dat

"Student debt is crushing the lives of millions of Americans. How does it happen that we can get a home mortgage or purchase a car with interest rates half of that being paid for student loans? We must make higher education affordable for all. We must substantially lower interest rates on student loans. This must be a national priority."

-Senator Bernie Sanders

You are probably looking at your massive student loans right now, thinking to yourself, *"How the heck did I take this much money out? This is the price of a freaking house".* The sad reality is that the average optometry student takes out a whooping average of $200,000 for optometry school and will likely be in debt for the next 20 years of his or her life.

The United States' student debt crisis **exceeds $1.3 trillion** for 2018 and has been an epidemic in society, shunting the growth of many young professionals. This indirectly forces new and bright doctors to live at home with their parents longer because they cannot afford to pay rent or begin to even think about buying a house. This in turn delays our younger generation in starting a family simply because they can barely take care of their own finances.

What do most optometrists normally do? Sadly, pay the minimum amount for 20+ years, hoping that our government will miraculously forgive their loans after 20-25 years. This is unfortunately the norm. Don't be normal, normal sucks! Normal people don't get rich or become wildly successful.

It is okay. Take a deep breath. Relax. I know it feels overwhelming at times but we are going to help you through this. We are going to walk you through the 5 important guidelines in tackling your student loans.

1. **Learning how to Budget**

2. **Establishing an Emergency fund (3 to 6 months expenses)**

3. **Federal Government program Repayment Plans**

4. **How to Refinance into Private Loans**

5. **Paying off your student loans ASAP**

6. **Live like a student for a few years**

Learning how to Budget...like a Sexy Mofo

I know I know; budgets are boring and lame. But establishing a budget is the significant core of any personal finance game plan. I have met so many so-called "rich doctors" who drive into their office with their fancy TESLA car but confess to me that they are living paycheck to paycheck! ***Why?*** Because they don't know how much they spend each month.

The truth is simple, you cannot know how much to invest for retirement, pay off your student loans or save for other financial goals if you do not know how much you have left at the end of month.

Here are the Steps for Starting a Budget:

- **List ALL monthly Income** (W2, 1099 fill-in, side business income) at the beginning of each month
    - o **Note:** If your income is irregular and varies monthly (for example, During the holiday season, ODs usually

bring in more income), just take the average monthly income. From this, you can make an estimate.

- **List ALL your monthly FIXED Expenses**
  - Examples: Rent, house mortgage/property tax, utilities, car insurance, student loan + other consumer debt (credit card, car lease) minimum payments, health/disability insurance, and minimum retirement contribution.
  - **Note:** Retirement IRA/401K contribution should ideally be a minimum of 10% of the total gross salary while paying off student debt and ideally 20% once all debt is paid off.
- **List your monthly NEEDS Expenses**
  - Examples: Groceries, car (gas, parking and/or public transportation), basic home supplies,
- **List your monthly WANTS Expenses:**
  - Examples: Restaurants, fast food, entertainment (Netflix, concerts, Spotify), coffee, alcohol & bars, mobile phone, haircut/hygiene.
- **Total your monthly INCOME and monthly EXPENSES**
  - If your end result shows more incomes than expenses, then you are off to a good start. Use any extra to fund other financial goals

Sounds pretty simple right? So why do so many people fail to stick to their budget? The reason is that our society often *confuses* NEEDS with WANTS. Like "I need to have my Netflix account" or "I need that $5 Starbuck Frappuccino every morning to survive," rather than focusing on what I need for basic modern human survival.

This little budgeting exercise will help gauge what really matters. For the first month, *try to be more flexible* with each item section because you can always increase/decrease the allocated fund for the following month. Usually, it takes 2-3 months to get a fairly accurate budget, so don't be too discouraged!

Review your budget monthly by looking at the previous month and which area you stay within range or which area you exceed in. Plan and adjust as needed (don't be a dummy and increase your entertainment budget by $500 because Coachella is coming up).

Here are three mobile applications that we highly recommend. All of which can link all your bank/credit card transactions
1. Mint.com (free)
2. YNAB.com "You need a Budget" (Free Trial but paid upgrade)
3. Everydollar.com (Free Trial but paid upgrade)

Establishing an Emergency fund (3-6 months Expenses)

Have you ever wondered to yourself, *"What if my car transmission breaks down? What if I break my arm and I am forced to do one-handed eye exams? What if I lose my job and cannot find a new one?"*

All of these "What if" situations can happen at any time and cause devastating results to our livelihood, usually forcing many Americans to get into further debt or even worse, bankruptcy.

This is where the importance of having a solid emergency fund comes in. It is basically an "Oh CRAP" fund that helps you sleep better at night. It is a way for you to financially prepare for all the worst things that can or will happen in life. We as doctors are so calculative in our thinking, that we expect everything to go perfectly as planned but life is filled with unexpected surprises that can cause us to be financially ruined.

On a positive note, optometrists overall have a fairly high job security because we can always pick up fill-in shifts at random offices to cover some of our expenses, or if needed, move to the middle of nowhere where our salary is likely to double.

But ideally, many people need a of *minimum of 3 months of expenses coverage* (not 3 months of income), but some can go a little bit lower if they have families close by (like their parents) to help them with financial trouble.

You are probably asking right now; can I use a credit card for my emergencies? **NO! A credit card is NOT an emergency fund.** This is how many people get into gigantic consumer debt. Don't be like the rest.

What is Considered an Actual emergency?

This is where a lot of people get into trouble. A 50% off sale at Nordstrom is NOT an emergency! Wanting to buy the new iPhone X is NOT an emergency! Buying a new car is NOT an emergency! A financial emergency will usually devastate your financial situation if you are not adequately prepared.

As you become more financially suave and have a good budget in place, then you tend to have *significantly less* emergencies.

Paying off your student loans (and other non-mortgage debts) ASAP

Your massive student loan can easily be the most expensive thing you will ever purchase, second to likely match this is your house mortgage. The average student loan amount for high-earning professionals can easily surpass $180-220K. Dentists have it much worse, with an average debt of close to $300-400K.

First of all, get rid of that typical socially enforced attitude of *"Oh it is a good debt"*, *"Everyone has student loans, it is normal for me not to worry about it"* or *"I will just think of this as a 2nd house mortgage and keep it around for 20+ years"*.

This is what normal doctors do and most normal doctors are broke. Normal does not get you rich! **Debt is debt, Buddy!** You took out the money for school and yes, I know it sucks and you're kicking your 22-year-old naive self for getting into this mess, but learn from it and take responsibility for it as an adult.

A great goal is to have your entire student loan paid off *within 5 years of graduating.* I know this seems impossible, but some ODs have done it within 2 years of sheer focus and intensity. But everyone's situation is different; use some critical reasoning to assess your own personal factors and financial priorities/goal.

We are going to focus on just paying off *non-mortgage debts* like student debt, consumer credit debt and/or car lease payment first. We will discuss when to pay off the house mortgage later.

There are two popular methods in attacking your student debt and
- **The Snow-Ball Method**
- **The Snow-Avalanche Method**

Method #1: The Snow Ball

This method takes into account the *behavioral aspect* of debt. You simply list ALL your debts from **highest to lowest amount** (despite of how high the interest rate.... I know, shocking right?), then make the minimum monthly payment on all debts.

Then, you start at the very bottom (which has the smallest debt), and aggressively attack that smallest debt amount, while still making minimum payments on all other debts above. Once you finish up the smallest debt, you take all minimum payments that you would have used for that smallest debt, and apply it to the next highest-level debt. Then, you pay off that next debt with immense focus. Then, you simply *repeat until you reach the top*. Like a small debt-destroying snowball rolling on the mountain, getting larger and building momentum! Nice imagery, eh?

Why is this method so effective? Studies show that the snowball method uses the psychological factor behind paying off debt. The tiny bit of endorphin released that people feel after paying off smaller amounts help them to stay motivated and advance onto the next level.

Method #2: The Snow Avalanche

This method takes the opposite approach; it emphasizes the *mathematical* aspect of debt. Again, you simply list ALL your debts but from **lowest to highest interest rate** (despite of how high the amount of debt is). You pay the minimum monthly payment on all debt and then you start at the very bottom with the highest interest rate. Then you aggressively attack that debt while still making minimum payments on all other debts above.

Once you finish up that debt with the highest interest rate, you take the minimum payment that you used to pay for that debt, and apply it to the next highest interest debt. Then you simply repeat until you reach the top. Basically, like a large debt-destroying patch of snow sliding down the mountain, but getting smaller and less intense as it gets down to the bottom.

Why is this method so effective? The snow avalanche method basically promotes the cold-hard math in paying off debt. You should attack the debt with the highest interest rate first to save the most money - simple as that.

Which Method is Right for you?

It is entirely up to you. There is no wrong way. You save a little bit in interest using the snow avalanche method, but our goal is to finish up in less than 5 years anyway. So, you likely only save $800 in interest. That $800 saving is honestly insignificant, compared to the total $200,000.

Paying off debt is one of the most emotionally and mentally draining processes for anyone, so having small little victories matter a lot. If you lose motivation and give up easily, then use the snowball method. All in all, it doesn't matter, just get started.

Types of Federal Student Loans Programs

This is one of the hardest, and to be honest, *most confusing, decisions* when it comes your student loans. It is complicated as heck because government policies, especially when it comes to education, *change all the time.* What is true today (in 2019) may not be applicable 5-10 years later. Our goal for this section is to weigh all the pros and cons, risks and benefits to help guide you in making the appropriate decision for your own personal financial situation.

Okay, let's first define some basic student loans differences and talk about some of the available government programs.

Private Student Loans: Usually more expensive and higher interest rate (some greater >10%). Also, interest accumulates during school. Basically, considered the same as consumer credit debt or a business loan. Require good credit score or a cosigner if credit score is poor.

Federal Student Loans: Usually less expensive (as low as 6.8%) and have multiple government program benefits attached. Federal loans have a *grace period* while you are in school (at least half-time student) where you don't have to start paying back loans. If the federal loans are **subsidized** loans, then the government will pay your interest while you are in school. Some Examples are:

- **Direct Subsidized Loans and Direct Unsubsidized Loans**

- **Direct PLUS Loans** (for graduate and professional students or parents)

- **Federal Perkins Loans**

Types of Major Available Federal programs

1) Standard Repayment Plan: This usually defaults up to 10 years, or up to 25 years (Extended Repayment plan), with the same set amount of payment each month. They usually have the least amount of interest with the 10 years repayment period

2) Graduated Repayment Plan: Payments starts low and then gradually increase as time passes on during the loan duration. This means your payments will be highest at the end

3) Revised Pay As You Earn Repayment Plan (REPAYE): Automatically set your monthly payments to 10% of your discretionary income
1. <u>Discretionary income</u> is anything that you earn above 150% of the federal poverty level for your family size. If you are

married, your spouse's income will be included into the calculation, thus increasing your monthly payment.

4) Pay As You Earn Repayment Plan (PAYE): Similar to the REPAYE but your maximum monthly payment is 10% of your discretionary income. Payments will actually be lower if you have a high debt-to-income ratio but will never be higher than compared to the standard repayment plan.

4) Income-Based Repayment Plan (IBR): Similar to PAYE and REPAYE but your monthly payments will be 10-15% of your discretionary income. Payments are automatically recalculated each year based on your income and family size. Again, your spouse's income will count toward your total income.

5) Income-Contingent Repayment Plan (ICR): Similar to IBR but have a higher monthly payment which is 20% of your discretionary income or fixed amount within 12 years duration, whichever is lesser.

6) Public-Service Loan Forgiveness (PSLF): Started in 10/2007, doctors working for non-profit organization such an Indian health reservation, tax-exempt hospitals such as the VA hospital or teaching hospitals for 10 years. Usually only IBR/PAYE/REPAYE/ICR repayment plans with 120 qualifying payments while employed full time (30 hours/week min) can qualify.

Here are 3 Great Benefits that we want to acknowledge with these federal programs:
1. Flexible repayment plans which can be easily changed during time of hardship
2. Assuming there is no co-signer attached, if a borrower passes away or has full/partial disability, all federal loans will be forgiven.
3. If you declare bankruptcy, your federal student loans will still NOT be dismissed. The government will have the power to garnish of any future paycheck earned.

What about Student Loan Forgiveness?

Okay, let's talk about the huge mythical elephant in the room which is Student Loan Forgiveness. Started in 10/2007, there are basically *three situations* where a doctor might get all their federal student loans forgiven.

1) Professionals who are doing income-based repayment (IBR) for **25 years** (or 300 monthly payments).
    a) A massive tax bill (taxed at ordinary income) for the total amount of loan forgiven will be due
2) Professionals who are doing pay-as-you-earn Repayment (PAYE, or REPAYE) for **20 years** (or 240 payments).
    a) A massive tax Bill (taxed at ordinary income) for the total amount of loan forgiven will be due
3) Professionals working full time in non-profit under Public service loan forgiveness (PSLF) for **10 years** (or 120 payments).
    a) No Tax bill is due on the loan forgiven.

Here is something to consider: you still have to pay tax on any loan forgiven which is a *huge financial tax burden.* Let's do an example and work out the math:

Dr. Normal has a typical student loan debt of $200,000 at an interest 6.8%. She is making a $100,000 salary and decides to do IBR (10%) with a hopeful 25-years loan forgiveness, which means her monthly payment is only $833. So, after 25 years passed, she is only paying $249,900, which is barely enough to *cover the $340,000 total Interest* payment that accumulated during the loan duration.

She is not even attacking the principle amount of $200,000. So, in the end, she is still left with a total student loan amount of *$90,100 interest left + $200,000 original loan = $290,1000.*

Assuming the same income bracket of 32% for high-earning doctors, she will get smacked with a **Tax Bill of $92,832.** This basically means **she ends up paying $342,732** (almost 1.75x the original amount).

I know shocking right?? The math doesn't even work out! I am all for the support of the good old U-S-A, but that is a LOT of trust to pay in our government for 25 freaking years. Also, under the fine print, not all federal loans will get approved (such as the federal family education loan). You must consider the fact that educational budgets/program and tax laws get changed all the time. Every new white house administration will run its policies differently. Who know what new orange-colored fanatic will be the next president.

Now let imagine the WORST-CASE SCENARIO. What if somehow the program gets eliminated?

Dr. Normal is stuck with a $342,732 student loan bill with NOTHING to show for it after 25 years. Furthermore, there are just too many rigid moving gears within each program and this is the perfect storm waiting to happen.

Under the 10 years Public Service Loan Forgiveness (PSLF) program, you need to be full time for a non-profit. What if you get sick or go on maternity leave, and need to be part time? Technically, then the program won't count repayment made, each month that you are considered "part time".

Also, you need to make 240-300 qualifying payments. What if you miss one IBR payment due to some financial emergency? Or, if you decide 10 years down the line, you want to aggressively pay off student loans sooner due to an increase in income or trying to obtain pre-approval for a home mortgage loan (which assesses your debt to income ratio).

As we began to write this book at beginning of 2019, we figured that at least a few professionals who started the 10 years PSLF program back in 10/2007 should have their loan forgiven in 10/2017. We have scoured every news outlet and financial blog online; we found ONE single person who got their loan forgiven via the PSLF. We did unfortunately find multiple PSLF lawsuits made by borrowers against loan providers for misleading information of what a non-profit is defined as or delay in qualifying payments. These hard-working professionals are basically screwed and have to restart their loan payment with nothing to show for the last 5-10 years.

The takeaway is, a lot of things in life can happen in 25 years! You cannot predict the future, no matter how well-prepared you think you are. The simple point, *being in debt for 25 years significantly limits your wealth building.*

How to Refinance into Private Loans?

This might be one of the most hotly debated topics among optometrists mainly because it is a ONE-time decision. Once you decide to refinance your federal loans into a private lender, you unfortunately cannot go back. You lose all the perks of federal programs like flexible repayment plan like income-based during time of hardships. But for many doctors, it is a no-brainer to refinance to a lower interest rate to save money.

Let first analyze the difference between two financial terms, because they often get confused:

- **Consolidating:** When you go through a *federal lender* to "combine" all your student loans together so you can make one easy payment. All your interest rates are averaged and this average is your final rate (it might be higher or it might slightly lower). This helps with the convenience of having one single payment.
- **Refinancing:** Like consolidating but you go through a *private lender,* which then "combines" all the student loans and restarts the loan term payment duration into a *significantly lower* interest rate. Therefore, it is better to refinance compared to consolidating.

Let's talk about some of the benefits on refinancing a typical 6.8% federal loan to private loans:

1. **Save money due to lower Interest (Range 4.5% to 1.9% depending which banks)**
   a. Example: If Dr. Strange has $200,000 at 6.8%, and was able to get a refinanced rate of 2.5%, he would save a total of $8600 that first year alone - that could go toward principal payment. Now imagine a 20year student loan - you would save a total of $112,049 in interest alone ($166,402 at 6.8% interest vs $54,353.09 at 2.5% interest). That is more than half of the actual principal amount that you are saving in interest! It essentially makes your 20 years loan into less than 10 years.
2. **Cash Bonus (along with Referral Bonus)**
   a. In addition to the huge savings in interest, many banks will offer a cash bonus of $300-$600 for signing up. Also, if you refer other colleagues, you can get an additional referral bonus.

3. **Easy Application process and Better Service from Lenders**
   a. If you have all the financial documents, most applications can be done online. Also compared to the service that you are getting from your federal lender; most private lenders want to keep your business and will strive to provide the best customer services and answer any questions you will have.

How do you actually Re-finance your Federal Loans?

Unlike a federal loan, there are some qualifications that you have to meet to be approved and here are some steps to get you started:

Step 1) Select the amount of Federal loans that you want to refinance.
- Most doctors refinance the whole amount to keep it simple.

Step 2) Get all your financial documents gathered. There are many factors that will get you approved and each bank have its own criteria.

- **Total student loan amount:** Ideally, most banks want a lower debt to income ratio, typically 2:1. So if your student debt is $200,000, your yearly income should ideally be $100,000.
- **Total annual income salary (including any fill-in 1099 income):**
  - ○ **Note:** While you can get a spouse or family member to *co-sign* your refinanced loan to help your chance of getting approved (assuming they have no major debt), there is significant risk, because essentially your massive student debt becomes their debt.
- **Total Monthly Expenses + Rent (which is a significant factor).** If you live at home with your parents or rent a cheap room, you are more likely to get approved
- **Credit Score (ideally >750)**
  - ○ Get a Free Report: Creditsesame.com or CreditKarma.com
- **Total amount of savings in checking (recommended 10-20% of total student debt)**
  - ○ **Note:** This is where it gets kind of iffy. For example, if you have $200,000 in debt, ideally most lenders want you to have 10-20% of debt in your saving/checking account. So, the minimum amount would be $20,000. I know this is difficult for most new graduates, so you might need to save up for a year (such as reduce retirement contribution or aggressive loan payment) or borrow money from family before applying to get approved.

Step 3: Select the bank with the best and <u>lowest </u>rate that you want to work with (all are available online)
- Private Student Refinancing lenders:
  - ○ *Earnest.com, Sofi.com, FirstRepublic.com, CommonBond.com, LendKey.com, Credile.com, SplashFinancial.com, ELFI.com, Linkcapital.com, LaurelRoad.com*
- Some lenders have specific requirements such being in close proximity to their local banks

- **Short (5-7 years) and variable term rate** *a*re the best deal with the lowest interest rate. The lowest rate that we have ever seen was 1.95% for a 5-year variable through First Republic (2019).

What Term Duration Amount Should I select?

Obviously, if you select a short-duration loan (5 years vs 10 years), you will get a much better rate, but your monthly payment will be significantly more. Example: Assuming a 200K student loans, comparing a 5 year at 1.95% vs 10 years at 2.6%, your required monthly payment will be $3,501 vs $1,894 *(HUGE DIFFERENCE).*

While the *lower interest rate is very attractive,* it is extremely important to make sure the required monthly payment is within your budget. We usually recommend starting with a safer term of *10-year duration.* You can always refinance to a shorter term like 5 years if circumstances change. Strive to pay extra payments each month.

Usually if you are a dual-income family (with your spouse having no debt) with a low budget, high income, and/or extremely motivated to live like a student for 5 years to pay off debt, then you will be done with your student debt within 2-5 years (Yes, it is possible! Quite a few of members in our *ODs on Finance* Facebook Group have accomplished this, along with the authors of this book)

Deciding between Variable versus Fixed rate

A fixed rate means whatever the rate is at the current moment is guaranteed to be the *same rate* during the next 10 years.

A variable rate will be lower initially but have a risk of either increasing or decreasing, depending on federal rate percentage changes during the next 10 year. Just think of a fixed rate, as *"insurance against increasing rates"* and your "premium" is the higher interest rate. *Fixed is usually better* but it doesn't make much of a significant difference mathematically if we finished up within 5 years.

Once approved, make it your goal to make any extra payments in addition to the required monthly refinanced payment. *Make it your financial goal to pay it off <u>within 5 years.</u>*

What are some Negatives about Refinancing?

Let's talk about the ***downsides of refinancing your student loans.*** First of all, as mentioned above, you <u>lose all the federal program benefits</u> such as flexible repayment during time of hardships, loan forgiveness due to disability or death, etc. This is a significant factor when you have a life-threatening life condition as a doctor, in which, we would *NOT recommend* refinancing your loans.

Most private bank lenders will have a one-time, one-month "grace" for time of financial hardship if you miss a single payment but you will automatically default and your credit score significantly suffers. This is definitely something to consider when you are applying for a house mortgage or private practice business loan.

In addition, *your student debt essentially become consumer debt* (similar to credit card) which means it will be *100% wiped out with a complete Chapter 7 bankruptcy*, giving the debtor a fresh start. But the downside is that unlike federal loans, even if you pass away, the bank will be able to take away your post-death "estate value" such as 401K/IRA/rental investment and try to re-claim any remaining debt. This will leave little for your heirs.

This is even worse when your spouse co-signs your refinanced student loan. Your student loan doesn't die with you, but instead becomes THEIR DEBT. This is why we don't recommend cosigning unless you completely understand the risks involved and your financial situation is extremely dire.

Summary

The most important upside in refinancing your student loans from 6.8% to 2.5% is that it allows you to have flexibility in your financial priorities. Perhaps, you can max more retirement accounts now before paying extra on student loans. But don't ever get into the illusion that you've done anything about your student debt.

Many doctors have the illusion that once they are done refinancing, they have "done something" and subsequently treat themselves to a fancy vacation. Yes, you made a smart mathematical move (*Bravo to you *Slow clap*)* but you still have your debt. Saving 2-3% in interest doesn't defeat the ugly huge $200,000 monster that is Sallie Mae.

Also, you are an adult. *It irks me so much when doctors play victim -* blaming the government or loan provider for their huge debt. Yes, I do agree that it is fiscally irresponsible to have a naive 18-year-old student approved for hundreds of thousands of dollars of student debt without the proper financial education. **Most definitely!**

But did someone hold a gun to your head and force you to take out those loans or attend some fancy private school in a high-cost of living state? **Most definitely not!**

Don't be a victim.

You can whine and complain all you want, but it is not going to change anything, your student debt is still there. Take control of your finances; make it a goal for you to pay off your student loans within 5 years. It is extremely hard work but it is definitely better than living a life of debt.

That was a long chapter. You finally made it to the end! When we were writing this book, we wanted to focus a lot of research and information about this topic because it is most likely the biggest financial (maybe even personal) stressor in most doctors' lives. We wanted our readers to be aware of all the financial pitfalls, and avoid all the dumb mistakes of student debt. We wanted to give you strategies on how to attack it in the most efficient way.

I will end this chapter with a positive take-way (you know that "Hamburger Technique" that you learn back in clinical methods to give patients bad news) but maybe; this chapter is more bread than prosciutto. But the most important thing is to:

Stay motivated!

This is one of the hardest things you will do in your life, and some days it will tear you down emotionally, leave you feeling helpless and crying in the corner of your exam, while some others days, you feel like Wonder Woman! Hopefully it is the latter. Keep track of your progress each month; it is okay to do small celebrations after your pay off each $5-10,000.

Definitely take a well-deserved and long vacation (but don't go into more debt) when you are done with your student loans. Gain support by talking to fellow colleagues and friends who are going through the same thing because they will keep you accountable and on track if you ever drool over that shiny new BMW for too long.

YOU GOT THIS! You made it through Optometry school; this is just one small obstacle to face.

CHAPTER FIVE: Finding the Right Career for You BY: Aaron

""Know yourself. Don't accept your dog's admiration as conclusive evidence that you are wonderful."

-Ann Landers

We will discuss finding meaningful employment as an optometrist in this chapter. We will touch the important aspects of resume building, online reputation, and interviewing. We will also discuss different modalities of practice and how their compensation differs. If you are past this stage in your career or think that you already have a good grasp on it, feel free to skim or skip this chapter.

So, you finally made it. You passed all your board exams. You made it through each internship and rotation (that VA one was a doozy!). You've got that nice, big diploma that now needs a frame. Four years of straight up grinding and you are finally done. Ok, so now what?

Realistically, you have three options: find a job, go into residency, or participate in something completely unrelated to optometry. Our sincere hope is that you choose one of the two first options. If you decide to forgo your residency, or if you just finished residency and are struck with the "So now what?" question, you will realize that the optometry world is your oyster.

But how do you find that pearl? It starts with preparation.

The Initial Search

The first step in finding meaningful employment is to actually find a job to apply to. So how does one go about doing this? When it comes to optometry you have a variety of options. Online listings including local Optometry schools and Optometry society websites will give you a good starting point. General employment websites such as indeed.com and monster.com are also valuable resources.

An important part of job searching, especially in the professional spectrum, is **networking.** Meeting other individuals in your industry face to face allows a web of connections to form. Spending five minutes with someone can be far more valuable than any words on a piece of paper.

You may have heard the saying "it's not what you know, it's who you know." In the job searching world, this rings absolutely true. Not every individual will provide you a direct path to your dream job, but many can help pave the road there by either referring you to talk to others or by recommending you to colleagues.

Networking also gets you connected to opportunities that may not exist in print. For example, you may run into an aging doctor who subconsciously would like an associate that will eventually buy his practice from him.

The passive idea might have been sitting in the back of his mind, but not activated until he had an interaction with a young doctor like you! (this is actual how my career as a practice owner started)

Get yourself out there. Whether it be society meetings, CE events; or local meetings like Rotary, Chamber of Commerce or Lions. Talk to everyone; be poised and professional while you do it. Let everyone you talk to know your objective, but do not hit him or her over the head with it. Ease yourself into comfortable conversation. Last, but not least, give them something to remember you by. Always keep those business cards handy before you bid farewell.

Build Your Case

Before you venture out into the exciting job market world, you need a solid basis. You need to appear as a brilliant and pristine young doctor that will bring exceptional patient care and immense profitability to wherever you go. You need to be King Midas of refraction and dilated fundus exams.

Wait, that's a little crazy!

You're right, it is, but the problem is: everyone else is trying to be King Midas too, so how can you *be different?*

Web and Social Media Presence

In order to be a stand out amongst the competition, a polished resume is vital. However, in this day and age, your online presence is arguably an even bigger factor in gaining employment. Spend a good amount of time on your LinkedIn page and any other social media-type professional profiles you may possess. Make sure you have a solid and succinct description on each page that highlights your professional prowess as well as the personality you'll present to both patients and co-workers alike.

Side note: If you think you are "above" professional social media or believe that it will not help you, you are going to get left behind. Lacking an account in this age of information technology shows two things:

(1) you are stubborn towards embracing innovation, and (2) possibly incompetent when it comes to technology - so in short, just make an account!

Network with as many individuals in your professional and geographic sphere as possible, even if you do not necessarily know them on a personal level. Create content that can provide value and entertainment to others if you chose to publicly post to gain attention. Finally, USE A **PROFESSIONAL PICTURE** on each and every one of your profiles. Our industry still favors professionalism over individualism. Take that statement how you like, but having an awesome application thrown out because you chose a picture of yourself at the top of Half Dome rather than in a suit is something that can happen, but can be easily avoided.

Speaking of Social Media, make sure all your personal pages including Facebook, Instagram, and Twitter are clean and professional looking. Employ privacy measures on your pages if necessary. Your Social Media accounts give a true look into your life and who you are as a person. Employers will frequently "stalk" these pages to gain personal insight on you. I have done it myself when looking to hire associate doctors for my practice.

Resume

Now that your online profiles flash brilliance and potential. It is time that your resume does so too. First thing is to make sure that your resume is short and sweet. If you think that a four-page resume is going to get you great offers, think again. If you are searching for your first job, it means you have zero professional experience. A resume over a page and half shows three things: (1) you fancy irrelevancy (no one cares about your high school decathlon, sorry), (2) you like to embellish (everyone did a rotation through ocular disease and we've all seen cataract surgery), and (3) you have issues with word economy. ***Moral of the story: keep the resume compact!***

Your compacted resume should be a quick highlight-reel of your accomplishments and acumen up to the present. Use aesthetically pleasing formatting and correct grammar; but keep in mind that your resume probably will not be picked apart. In fact, it will probably be glanced at, at best. If you are dealing with an individual/company experienced at hiring the best, the nitpicking will come during the interview.

Cover Letter

A cover letter is a necessary evil that should accompany your Resume. If you are applying to multiple positions, you will be tempted to make a template. Word to the wise, a template can be spotted from a mile away. Try to add as much personalization to the letter as you can. Remind the potential hiring personnel that you are human and not a robot. Most of all show the recipient what you can offer. Show that you can offer value and growth to whatever practice you are trying to join.

Interview

So now you finally made it past the on paper (and on screen) hoopla. You sold yourself well enough in text and pictures (professionally of course) to make it to a one-on-one meeting with someone that sees potential in you. The job is on the line, and it rests on your abilities to communicate.

Truth be told, the interview process is all about *selling you.* Your brand, your ethos, your bedside manner and your overall comprehension of the optometric field. All of this will be teased and dissected in your interview. So, what is the key to conveying that you are in fact the best candidate for the job? It lies in two easy steps.

1) Be Yourself

Be yourself. Really? Can you be more cliché? Nope. And there is a reason the phrase "be yourself" is cliché - it works! Sure, you can bullshit your way through an interview making grandiose claims that fall short of who you really are and what you can really offer and end up landing the best job ever. However, once you are in the job, that bullshit will quickly be sniffed out. No one can be an actor forever (also your Doctor of Optometry degree is a far cry from an acting school degree).

But there is a bigger issue than getting caught when it comes to bullshitting your way into a job. *You won't be happy.* Living up to a constant standard that you cannot meet is both tiresome and draining. I have had countless colleagues who have ended up in this position. Eventually, you get burned out. In the world of eye doctoring, burn out is dangerous and can lead to a complete downward spiral both mentally and emotionally.

By being yourself, you can connect with your future employer (and potential partner or associate) at a deeper level. Developing a sense of trust and honesty early in your relationship with colleagues will help you achieve more success down the line. Forming bonds of integrity between doctors and staff will help you grow as an individual, and will help those around you grow as well.

2) Be Confident

Be confident. Confidence goes a long way in any professional career. Optometry is no exception. When I look to employ an associate doctor, confidence carries over many other attributes. It shows competence and the ability to stand up and assert meaningful care both in practice and in personal situations. Confidence also comforts patients. Confidence in one's skill set and diagnosing allows the patient to feel confident in the practitioner. Many young doctors find that the first time patients stop questioning their amount of time in practice is not when they grow a few gray hairs, rather it is when they learn to make every statement and assertion with complete confidence.

What about overconfidence? Does such a thing exist for me as an optometrist? Of course, it does. Confidence comes with an internal *ownership* of your abilities and competence. When confidence is overstepped, it leads to two ugly stepsisters: arrogance and complacency. **Confidence** allows you to have faith in yourself, but introspective about your mistakes and shortcomings. **Arrogance and complacency** place you in a situation where you are blind to these shortcomings.

Leveraging Your Offers

When the hiring process happens, there are two sides that each have conflicting goals. The employer seeks to compensate the employee with an amount that maximizes his/her profitability while still sustaining the employee. The employee seeks to be paid the highest amount possible for the services/products that he/she will be rendering for the employer. This is where *leveraging* comes into play.

When negotiating with a future employer, don't instantly put pen to paper on the initial offer given. Start negotiations with your employer. Consider a higher pay rate, but also look into benefits, vacation and retirement plans if applicable. One of your biggest tools in negotiating will be leveraging other employment offers against the offer in question.

Don't compromise in your negotiation. The key to a successful negotiation is to arrive at terms that both you and your employer find favorable. Show empathy and understanding in your conversation with your future employer.

Here are 5 negotiating tactics that I have found to be very useful in the world of optometry (both as an employee to start with and later on as an owner), real estate and general finance situations such as obtaining business loans. These tactics are often referenced in books about negotiating:

1) Let the other party go first - This allows you to see the other party's hand before even playing the game and enables you to understand the other party's motives better

2) Let the other party do the majority of the talking - The more you talk, the more likely you are to release pertinent information on needs and release "tells." Often times, excessive talkers can actually talk themselves into a corner without any input from the opposing party.

3) Validate emotions and anchor them through labeling – During conversation, frequently validate emotions that your counterpart displays by repeating them back. This gives you a basis for your counter argument and cements the opposing party's opinions so that they cannot be changed.

4) Use ranges rather than hard numbers – When the other party asks you to initiate a salary number or the number of days off, first give a range with your lower number being your upper limit and the higher being a number you view to be impossible. This prevents you from hitting the proverbial early "wall"

5) When you feel it is time to reach a hard number – use an odd one – Using an odd number, or a number with a few options attached to it makes the other party believe that you used significant research and calculation to get to it and thus validates it more. Think about it, if you state that you would like a yearly salary of $147,000 plus a 12% production bonus alongside benefits and 12 days PTO, this seems a lot more astute than $160,000 per year.

Remember Supply and Demand

Supply and demand is the over-arching theme of Economics and thus can be applied to the economics of job hunting. If you are looking for a job in an area with a relatively scarce population of optometrists relative to overall population (often seen in rural communities), you should have no problem negotiating a position with high pay, since more of the overall *market share* for your community will belong to your employer's practice, and subsequently you. Hence, the demand for your skill-set strongly outweighs the supply.

On the contrary, if you look for work in an area saturated with optometrists, such as a big city; you will not only have a smaller *market share* (and less revenue as a provider), but you may also be *competing* for that sliver of market share. This allows potential employers to offer less compensation due to scarcity. In this case, the supply of optometrists much outweighs the demands.

Modalities of Practice

Admittedly, we just delved into a lot of philosophical and "self-help" material when describing how to prepare for an interview and land a job. While not overtly related to finances, landing a job is vitally important, because it will probably be the biggest contributor to your income. Now that we are past that, let us take a look at the different avenues you can take with your career path.

Employer vs. Employee

Although optometry itself is a specialized field, many different modalities of practice exist. The biggest overall differentiator is whether you plan to be an owner of a practice or if you plan to be employed. When you are working as an employee, keep in mind that the business employing you needs to make a profit and is using you as a revenue generator. If the business is not making money on top of your daily rate, then the business is not meeting its bottom line (this even applies if you are working at a nonprofit - overhead and other personnel costs need to be covered). ***Plain and simple, you will not be making your maximum potential as an employee.***

On the flip side, being an owner allows you to take a bigger piece of the pie. However, this pie comes with a few heavy grains of salt. In addition to being a doctor, you also become a business owner, which involves stress, and work that simply is not taught in school. You also become much more than the average doctor. After seeing patients, you are grinding numbers, making decisions, and disciplining staff. You constantly must find ways to keep your patient load, combat the competition, and most importantly, keep positive cash flow.

So how does ownership vs. employment measure up? In *Review of Optometry*'s article "2016 Income Survey: Things are Looking Up," it states "self-employed ODs averaged $197,533 [annual income], while employed ODs reported an average of $125,099—a 58% difference." If you are going to be a top earner in the industry, you should own a practice (or multiple practices).

Note: When we talk ownership, we refer to Private Practice. When you own or are involved in a partnership that owns a private practice, you (or your partnership) exude complete control over your business entity. This in turn matches the definition of business ownership.

Corporate subleases while appealing and marketed as practice "ownership" unfortunately cannot be classified as ownership due to the confines that the corporation places on the doctor. Instead, they represent a form of employment that allows the doctor certain financial decisions and freedoms.

Type of Practice Modalities

In this next section, we will go through each modality of practice. We will give a quick summary of the modality as well as its pros and cons both in terms of overall practice satisfaction and financial return.

Please note that in order to write this section I took a two-pronged approach: first, I referenced the most current (2017 data) salary surveys and second, I interviewed multiple optometrists from each modality to get firsthand information. My optometrist pool was equal parts male and female, graduating from ten different optometry schools and ranging in age from 28 to 64 years old.

1) Private Practice - Ownership

Being a private practice owner is often represented as the pinnacle or the gold standard of being a successful optometrist. It statistically places you in the slot of high earner and generally garners a fair amount of respect, but like everything that is too good to be true, there is a catch.

Practice ownership has to the potential to make you very rich or very poor. The deciding factor is a hodge-podge of variables including your skill as a practitioner, your acumen as a business owner, your drive as a proponent/marketer and just plain luck. Starting cold can be especially daunting. There may be a period of years where you would not produce a profit. And just like any other business, there is always the possibility of failure.

When you get past all the obstacles that make your stomach churn and keep you awake at night, you find that there are some luxuries to be had as a practice owner. You can make your own hours and you can pay yourself what you deem appropriate. Remember when we talked about a business needing to make money off of you as an employee and thus, they consistently undervalue you monetarily? This principle does not necessarily need to be applied for owning a practice.

2) Private Practice - Employee

Being an employed optometrist at a private practice puts you in a fair situation. Flexibility for negotiating your compensation seems to be at its max with private practice. Due to the lack of a corporate structure or a fledgling of ophthalmologists hovering over your head, you tend to have more leeway in your style of practice and your scope. Production bonuses are also commonplace in private practice, and if you are good, these can be very lucrative.

One of the biggest benefits of working in a private practice is the future possibility of purchasing the practice or becoming a partner. This possibility, if available, is something that should be clearly defined between you and the owner(s) of the practice *BEFORE or AT THE START of your employment.*

If you are in fact working in a practice with the possibility of later ownership, you have two jobs: 1) Be a fantastic optometrist and serve your patients well 2) Constantly watch and take notes on every nook and cranny of the office. (For an in-depth look into purchasing an existing practice, take a look at Chapter 10).

So, what are the cons of employed private practice work? It is possible to get low-balled for your compensation, especially if you are a new graduate or are in an over saturated area. Take for instance, a colleague of ours - an extremely smart, but completely naïve new graduate took a job that paid $250 a day in the Bay Area, CA. Unfortunately, this is far too common in highly saturated cities.

Additionally, if you had plans to take over the practice, but the owner thinks differently or you uncover some secrets you wish you did not see, your career could *essentially stagnate*, which probably will result in you looking for new employment.

3) Corporate - Employee/Sublease

Corporate optometry refers to optometry practiced in offices owned by large corporations, often referred to as chain stores. Large corporations generally own the optical section of the office and maintain control of glasses and contact lens sales. These corporations either sublease space to optometrists or employ optometrists based on state law. Subleasing involves renting a space in the corporation's store to an optometrist and taking either rent or a portion of exam fees (or both). Employment involves either a salary or hourly pay scale for performing exams.

Ease of sliding into productive practice probably best describes the corporate modality. Employment is relatively available, even in saturated cities. The icing on the cake is you normally get a pretty good starting rate. Taking a sublease in a high volume corporate office nearly guarantees a solid payday.

So, What are the Drawbacks?

Well, first of the all, there is an immense pressure to sell products. After all, the corporation is enlisting your services to help produce sales. This is part of the reason your starting salary will probably be pretty decent. However, you will soon learn that your pay rate really is not going to increase much. **Why?** Because the corporation does not have an economic need to do this. If you decide to quit because of stagnating pay, they will simply hire another optometrist. Unlike private practice, corporations generally rely on their brand image and promotions to keep their patient base, rather than familiarity of doctors.

Then, there is the *stigma of working corporate.* Many private practitioners and academics view the corporate model as a lesser form of optometry due to constrictions placed on practice scope by the corporation and the overarching pressure to be a salesman.

But is corporate optometry really the bastard child that relishes in conveyor belt refractions? Not necessarily. Practicing to your full scope and allowing your patients to experience exemplary care are within your reach. If you find yourself settling into a corporate optometry career, leverage your strengths and skills to not only benefit your patients, but also to make you a happier practitioner.

4) Academia

Before we even begin to discuss the financial pros and cons of practicing optometry in the academic setting, it is important to note that most individuals entering academia *do not have financials at the top of their priority list.* And rightfully so, professors and researchers enter their fields because they love what they do. They make new clinical discoveries and they enrich the minds of future practitioners.

That being said, if you do plan to enter Academia and have financial goals, it is important to know the facts. Amongst all the salary survey studies I looked at, Academia consistently ranks as the lowest paying. This makes sense considering the economics of running a nonprofit institution of higher education. Although tuition rates may be high, the school is always incurring losses, most notably in its clinics, where future doctors learn their trade by making mistakes over and over again. Although pay may be lower, benefits offered by academic institutions tend to be fairly good.

5) Hospital/PPOs, Veteran Affairs (VA) & OD/MD Centers

Working as an optometrist in a hospital, VA or OMD setting allows for a high exposure to medical optometry in a fast paced environment. Salary surveys point to these settings as averaging *slightly below* corporate and private practice. While growth may be slower in this setting, long-term commitment coupled with quality work may result in promotions to more lucrative positions such as clinical director.

Additionally, being in a medical setting allows an optometrist access to a network of expansion. Opportunities to be involved in research and lecture on the side (whether it be academia or pharma) are far more likely to pop up for someone inundated in medical cases.

6) Military

Entering into a military scholarship program presents an interesting conundrum for an optometrist. The idea behind a military scholarship is simple: you get your schooling paid for in exchange for providing your (eventual) doctor skills to the military for a set time period.

The positives with this modality are that you enter the workforce debt-free and have the honor of serving your country with your optometric skills. The negatives reflect in lifestyle and pay scale. There is a chance the military may place you in an area that you do not necessarily wish to live in. Additionally, the compensation for your "service time," normally 3 years, is quite a bit below the national average. This begs the question that if you took an "above average" job straight out of school, could you pay off your loans in the that three-year time span and end up with some extra cash?

Practice Modality	Pros	Cons
Private Practice - Owner	Highest income potential. You are your own boss Growth/expansion = more $	Most risky. High stress level. Extra work involved with ownership
Private Practice - Employee	Fair Income. Possibility of ownership	Set income at many places. "Stagnated career" if owner refuses to sell
Corporate	High starting income. Easy flow due to corporate structure. No worries about sales or insurance Relatively low requirements	Income plateaus quickly Lack of "respect" Frequently overbooked/overworked
Academia	Highly rewarding High level of respect for professors. Good benefits	Low income. Little room for wage increase. Higher requirements (residency and sometimes more)
Hospital/VA	Good Benefits. Interesting cases	Set income. Grueling schedules. Often in "shadow" of ophthalmology. Higher requirements

In conclusion, there are many different paths and decisions that you can make regarding your career that can drastically affect your financial well-being. Choosing your modality of practice and whether to remain employed or start ownership has long-term effects on your earnings and finances. Intangibles *such as your professionalism and demeanor affect your career and financial trajectory as well. My best advice to you is to find a balance.*

I think back to a quote that one of my late optometric mentors told me about running a successful practice and being a successful practitioner:

"Love your patients, care for your staff and work your ass off - the rest will follow."

You do not necessarily need to chase the money in order to make it, your passion for your craft will reward you greatly.

The Optometrist's Guide to Financial Freedom

CHAPTER SIX: Planning for Retirement BY: Dat

"Failing to plan is planning to fail"

- Benjamin Franklin

You are probably a new hotshot young doctor with a brand-new job, finally getting the big doctor salary paycheck. I know you probably want to live your life after being in school for over 8+ years. I mean you feel like you deserve it right??

I know you want to travel the world and live the "YOLO" lifestyle (The *"You Only Live Once" slang would probably not be cool anymore by the time this book is published in 2019*). But just as you spend all those years to plan your academic journey from college to optometry school, you need to **plan your retirement**. You are not going to be young forever my friend!

A lot of people have this giant misconception about retirement! The goal of retirement is NOT to sit on your butt all day and do nothing. The goal of retirement is be ***financially free***. Free to do what the heck you want to do, free to work part time, free to still see patients without the need for a paycheck, free to travel the world, free to donate to charities or volunteer, and free to follow a life-long passion that you put off! All while you don't have to worry about making enough money to eat or pay your bills.

That is the True Goal of retirement

There is a really sad story about an optometrist that I will share with you guys. It will always stick with me and personally started my own financial journey.

Back when I was a young doctor, I was working a fill-in day shift at LensCrafter in the Bay Area California. I met this super nice and slightly older Asian male doctor named Alan (roughly in his mid-70s) Alan was also working there on the same day with me and doing miscellaneous shifts at different offices around the area. Alan was so caring with patients but I could tell he had trouble physically moving around due to his age. I got to know him throughout the day while we double-teamed the patient load.

Then, I finally got the courage to ask, *"Hey Alan, if you don't mind asking me asking, no offense, but why are you still working at your age?"*

He quietly paused and sat down with a slight look of discouragement on his face: *"No worries Dat, I don't mind sharing. When I was a new graduate back, I was living in San Francisco paying for this luxurious apartment with super high rent. So I never got around to saving any money for retirement. I simply wanted to enjoy life so I went out a lot and travel a lot, and just blew all my money trying to live like a 'doctor'.*

Years passed as I continue living paycheck to paycheck. Then I got married and bought a fancy 'doctor' house without paying off much of my student loans. Then about a few years later, I needed a major surgery for my heart so I kept on accumulating more medical debt. Then my wife divorced me, which was a really hard phase in my life. I would have retire a long time ago but I still have my house mortgage to pay off and I don't simply have enough my retirements to support me and my children who are still in college right now"

I **numbly sat there** listening to his story. Alan got a little bit closer to me, *"Look Dat, you are young now, you still have time which is the greatest gift at this point in your life. But start preparing for your retirement because it will come sooner than you expect. I don't want you to make the same mistakes as me"*

That night, I went home and brought all the personal finance books that I can get my hand on. I will always take Alan's words to heart and it is a constant reminder why personal finance and funding retirement are very vital for young doctors.

So, if I haven't convinced you about the personal and emotional importance of retirement, I am going to show you the **math behind it.** Why save for retirement? Simple answer:

The Magic of Compounding Interest

You have probably heard this term so many times before! Basically, if you simply put a small amount today and let it stay there for 30 years, then it will exponentially grow each year.

	Smart Investor	Late Investor	Hard Investor
20			
25	14,369.15		
30	34,759.27		
35	49,324.10	14,369.15	14,369.15
40	69,991.88	34,759.27	34,759.27
45	99,319.87	49,324.10	63,693.25
50	140,936.87	69,991.88	104,751.14
55	199,992.23	99,319.87	163,013.10
60	283,792.96	140,936.87	245,688.00
65	402,707.86	199,992.23	363,005.32

Example: Let's look at 3 different doctor investors in this example. Doctor A is a *Smart investor*, Doctor B is the *Late Investor* and Doctor C is the *Hard investor*. Lets assume a typical **7% interest Market rate,** where the shaded dark area indicates the years in which a $200 a month was saved

Doctor A: *Smart Investor*, starts saving $200 per month at age 25 until he is 35 years old, then stop all contributions. He invest for a total of 10 years

Doctor B: *Late Investor* starts saving $200 per month at age 35 until he is 45 years old then stop all contributions. He invest for a total of 10 years

Doctor C: *Hard Investor* starts saving at $200 per month at age 35 until he retires at 65 *(Typical retirement age). He invests for a whooping duration of 30 years while contributing the most money over his lifetime.*

At the time of retirement age which is 65 years old for all three investors, we can see a few surprising results:

- By simply investing earlier at Age 25 (10 years before the Late Investor), the **Smart Investor has <u>DOUBLE</u> the amount compared to the Late Investor** ($402,707 compared to $199,992).
- The Hard investor started saving at Age 35 (10 years behind Smart Investor) and even though he tries to catch up and tried to save an extra $200 per month until he retires at 65 years ago. The Hard Investor still has *$39,702.54 less than Smart Investor ($363,0005 vs $402,707).*
- In addition, the Hard Investor put in **more *time and thus more*** money contributions compared to the shorter investing time by Smart Investor (30 years vs 10 years).

The moral of the story? The sooner you start saving the quicker you will see power of compound interest.

How Much Do I need for Retirement?

Now that I impress you with the magic potential of compounding, how much do we really need in retirement?? Go ahead, think of a number. $50,000? $100,000? $750,000? You are probably way off! As a general guideline, most people need:

> **25 x Post-Retirement Expenses = Total** amount Needed in their retirement funds

This rule assumes a few educated factors:
1) Average Market return of 7%
2) Retirement age of 65 years old with a 30 years life span longevity
3) No debts such as credit card, house mortgage and student loans in retirement
4) Doesn't include social security (~average of $20,000 per year in 2019) mainly because we never want to fully rely on the government because taxes policies change all the time.
5) No other side business income
6) Assuming a safe *4% withdrawal rule*

What the Heck is 4% rule?

Basically, the Trinity study states that a person in retirement can safely withdraw 4% of their retirement funds without significantly reducing the total principle amount, thus accounting for yearly inflation of 3% (*yes, I know inflation sucks*) with an average of 7% market gains.

Example: Dr. McSizzle is 65 years old and is planning to retire. He is completely debt-free with a paid-off house mortgage. His health is getting worse so is his health insurance is significantly higher compared to his 20s. He needs an annual income of $80,000 to maintain his current lifestyle and yearly expenses. He also wants enough to travel and spend time with his grandkids. So, following the 25x Rule, he would need a total of:

$2 million or ($80,000 yearly expenses x 25)

I know that is quite shocking to believe but the sad reality is that the average American only have *$91,000 in their retirement funds by 65 year old*. If we break down the math over 30 years, assuming an average market gain of 7%, the average American *only save $23 per* *month toward retirement.* That is more than you spend in a week on coffee!

What is the Latte Factor?

There is a famous theory out there called the **Latte factor**. It simply emphasizes the power of compounding from small daily expenses such as a $4 coffee latte. If we take that $4 coffee per day x 365 days, then comes to a whooping total of $1460 per year. If we were to invest that $1460 from age 30 to 65 years old, using a conservative market return of 7% per year, then that daily cup of coffee will be worth a *mammoth $214,770 at 65 years old.*

Now, I am not picking on coffee but I do want to emphasize that tiny expenses add up and it honestly doesn't take much per month to save up for retirement.

What about Social Security?

"Social security was never intended to be a retirement plan. At most, it was designed to provide an income supplement." -David Bach

Sorry to break your bubble, little buddy! But right now, the future of the Social Security program is largely unknown. It is estimated that by 2033, the government will **only be able to pay 77% of all current** Social Security recipients. This means that younger workers will likely end up getting a *much lower monthly reimbursements* compared to the older Baby Boomer generations, as time progresses.

With the advancement in healthcare, people are living significantly longer past the average life expectancy of 76 years old (male) and 81 years old (female) and the government is simply not prepared for that.

But even assuming that social security benefits will be paid out in full, don't expect much! For a typical optometrist making an average $120,000 salary and paying taxes, they should have an expected *monthly benefit check of around estimated $2,295 in retirement.* That is only a yearly income of $27,540, way below the poverty level in USA and it will definitely not account for inflation in retirement age.

So basically, don't rely on Social Security to support your retirement. If it happens and you get some benefit, then great! Just think of it as extra gravy on top!

How much should I save up each month toward Retirement?

This is a very personal choice because everyone's financial situation is so different. We always recommend investing in tax-protected accounts like 401K or IRAs starting out with **10-15% minimum of your total GROSS SALARY**, and **ideally 20-25%** once you are done with all non-mortgage debt like student debts, credit card debt or car loans (Don't worry, we will give you a guideline on list of financial priorities in a later chapter).

Doing that initial 10-15% toward retirement will really get you a boosting start due to compounding magic while you are aggressively paying off your student debt.

Example: Dr. Retina is 30 years old and is making $100,000 salary as a new young optometrist. If he is able to fully contribute both of his 401K plan through his employer (max contribution up to $19,000) and also wisely open up a Roth IRA (max contribution up to $6,000). This means he is contributing *$25,000 a year (or 25% of his income)* toward retirement. Assuming a 7% return and retirement age of 65 y/o, he will have close to $3.7 million in his retirement account.

So how much will Dr. Retina have to spend per year in retirement? So if we use the 25x rule mentioned above which again is:

25 x Post-Retirement Expenses = Total amount Needed in their retirement funds

This means that Dr. Retina will have a yearly income of $147,889 to use during retirement. CRAZY AMOUNT right?? He can balla out as much as he want!

What if we use the same number but with a lower saving rate?

Example: Dr. Conjunctiva is *only doing 10% contribution.* During retirement, Dr. Conjunctiva will have roughly $1.12 Million or a yearly expense of $45,000.

This conservative example shows us what a minimum 10% retirement contribution on a doctor's salary can truly accomplish. Most high-earning doctors can easily max out all their retirement account limits, especially if they are debt-free!

Selecting the right Retirement plan for you:

Okay, let get technical real fast and define all the different types of retirement plans out there first before we dive into which one ideally works best for your financial situation. *Check out the Retirement chart and refer back as needed.*

Remember our goal is maximize all the tax benefits for our high-income salary in whatever tax situation we are in. For example: Employed W2 or Independent contractor 1099 or Business owner.

There are 8 Basic Types of Retirement Plans Offered (2019)

1. **Employer-provided 401K (Private), 403B (Hospital/Academic Setting) or 457B (Government)**

2. **Traditional Individual Retirement Account (Trad-IRA)**

3. **Roth Individual Retirement Account (Roth-IRA)**

4. **Solo/Individual 401K**

5. **Employer-provided Saving Incentive Match Plan IRA (SIMPLE-IRA)**

6. **Self-employed IRA (SEP-IRA)**

7. **401K with Profit-Sharing Plan (PSP)**

8. **Defined Benefits Plan (DBP)**

	Employer-Provided 401K/403B/457B
Who?	Company-provided account for Employees
Contributions	Can contribute **Pre-Tax Deductible dollar** up to **$19,000** (Extra $6,000 catch-up for > Age 50. Employer automatically deduct pre-tax contributions on your paycheck
Taxes	All withdrawals are taxed at income rate after age 55 but additional 10% Penalty imposed if withdrawal made before retirement age 55
Pros:	-Roth option may be available depending on your employer -Usually have an employer match (1-10%) -Able to borrow money as 5-years loan (limited to 50% of 401K fund or $50,000, whichever is less) -Able to withdraw without penalty due to hardship such as disability and high medical expense
Cons:	-Funds selection may be great or very poor. Fund cost can vary in price or have high administration account yearly fees depending on company -Must leave previous company to roll-over to another 401K with new employer or roll-over into personal IRA
	Traditional Individual Retirement Account (Trad-IRA)
Who?	Any earned-income individual (W2 or 1099)
Contributions	Can contribute up to **$6,000 Pre-tax Deductible dollars** (Extra $1,000 catch-up for >Age 50). Will have **Modified Adjusted Gross income (MAGI)** limit if already have a main employer retirement plan Single: Max MAGI income= $74,000 (start to phase out contribution level at $64,000) Married filing jointly: Max MAGI income = $123,000 (start to phase out contribution level at $103,000)
Taxes	All withdrawals are taxed at income rate after 59 ½ but additional 10% Penalty imposed if withdrawal made prior to retirement age
Pros:	-Easy to set up with great fund choices -Able to withdraw without penalty due to hardship such as disability and high medical expense -Able to withdraw without penalty for qualified Higher education (You, your spouse or your children or grandchildren) -Able to withdraw without penalty up to $10,000 per spouse for 1st home purchase (You, spouse, grandparents or children/grandchildren)
Cons:	-Low contribution Limit

	Roth Individual Retirement Account (Roth-IRA)
Who?	Any earned-income individuals (W2 or 1099)
Contributions	Can contribute up to **$6,000 Post-tax Deductible dollars** (Extra $1,000 catch-up for >Age 50). Single: Max MAGI income= $137,000 (start to phase out contribution level at $120,000) Married filing jointly: Max MAGI income = $199,000 (start to phase out contribution level at $189,000)
Taxes	-Contributions (what you put in) can be withdraw at any time, without taxes or penalty -If you withdraw earnings (a.k.a. gains) before age 59 ½ then it will be taxed as income tax rate +10% penalty. Otherwise, withdrawal on gains will be tax-free after 59 ½
Pros:	-Easy to set up with great fund choices -Able to withdraw EARNING without penalty due to hardship such as disability and high medical expense -Able to withdraw EARNING without penalty for qualified Higher education (You, your spouse or your children or grandchildren) -Able to withdraw EARNING without penalty up to $10,000 per spouse for 1st home purchase (You, spouse, grandparents or children/grandchildren)
Cons:	-Low contribution Limit -Max *Income limit, but able to do Backdoor Roth IRA*
	Solo/Individual 401K
Who?	Self-employed 1099 individual or Business owner with no employees (other than spouse)
Contributions	Can contribute **Pre-Tax Deductible dollar** $19,000 toward the employee/employer's 401K, along with an employer match/contribution of $37,000, equaling **$56,000 (or Max 25% of total income)**
Taxes	All withdrawals are taxed at income rate after age 55 but additional 10% Penalty imposed if withdrawal made before retirement age
Pros:	-Able to borrow money as 5-year loan (limited to only 50% of 401K or $50,000, whichever is less). -Able to withdraw without penalty due to hardship such as disability and high medical expense
Cons:	-Harder to set up and require a plan administer like Vanguard

Saving Incentive Match Plan IRA (SIMPLE-IRA)	
Who?	Business with <100 employees or self-employed individuals
Contributions	Can contribute **Pre-Tax Deductible Dollars** up to **$13,000** (Extra $3,000 catch-up for > Age 50)
Taxes	All withdrawals are taxed at income rate after 59 ½ but Additional 10% Penalty imposed if withdrawal made prior to retirement age
Pros:	-Able to withdraw without penalty due to hardship such as disability and high medical expense -Able to withdraw without penalty for qualified Higher education (You, your spouse or your children or grandchildren) -Able to withdraw without penalty up to $10,000 per spouse for 1st home purchase (You, spouse, grandparents or children/grandchildren)
Cons:	-No Roth Option.
Self-employed IRA (SEP-IRA)	
Who?	Self-employed 1099 individual or small business owner (including those with employees)
Contributions	**Pre-Tax** Deductible **dollar for 1099 income.** Can contribute up to $56,000 (max is 25% of income). You simply claim the deduction when you file taxes on your 1099 income Employer of SEP IRA can offer it to their employees and thus automatically deduct pre-tax contributions on your paycheck or you can deduct it during tax filing.
Taxes	All withdrawals are taxed at income rate after 59 ½ but additional 10% Penalty imposed if withdrawal made before retirement age
Pros:	-Easy to set up with great fund choices -Able to withdraw without penalty due to hardship such as disability and high medical expense -Able to withdraw without penalty for qualified Higher education (You, your spouse or your children or grandchildren) -Able to withdraw without penalty up to $10,000 per spouse for 1st home purchase (You, spouse, grandparents or children/grandchildren)
Cons:	-No Roth Option.

401K with Profit-Sharing Plan (PSP)	
Who?	Employer-provided 401K along with a Profit Sharing feature where the employer can make a profit-sharing contribution to employees. Ex: Group of doctor partners
Contributions	Can contribute **Pre-Tax Deductible dollar** up to **$19,000 (401K) + $56,000 (max is 25% of participant salary)**
Taxes	All withdrawals are taxed at income rate after age 55 but additional 10% penalty imposed if withdrawal made before retirement age
Pros:	-Significant higher Benefits and higher contribution in short period of time, leading to subsidized early retirement
Cons:	-Extremely expensive and overly Complicated. -Need an administer and cannot discriminate toward higher-paying participants
Defined Benefit Plan (DBP)	
Who?	-Small Business with no employees other than the owners and spouses. -Basically employer-sponsored that pays out monthly benefits upon retirement based in a set formula
Contributions	Employers can only contribute **Pre-Tax Deductible dollars up to $225,000 (or max 100% of average income for 3 highest constructive years)**
Taxes	All withdrawals are taxed at income rate after age 59 ½ but additional 10% Penalty imposed if withdrawal made before retirement age -Upon retirement, can be paid out in 3 ways such as (1) single life annuity (Fixed monthly benefit until you die, but no further payment to your family survivors upon death), (2) Qualified joint/survivor annuity (your surviving spouse will get benefits until his or her death) or (3) Lump-sum payment.
Pros:	-Significant higher Benefits and higher contribution in short period of time, leading to subsidized early retirement
Cons:	-Extremely expensive and overly Complicated. -Need an administer to prevent an Excise Tax if minimum contribution requirement is not satisfied

What is the Difference Between Roth vs. Traditional?

Now that we have a broad understanding of the different retirement plans, let's talk about the differences for Roth versus Traditional that can apply to either a 401K or IRA. This is basically how the government can tax our retirement accounts by forcing you to pay money in taxes now (pre-Tax) and later on (post-Tax). Either way, the house aka "IRS Government" will get its cut. This can get complicated, so just *breathe and read carefully.*

Simply put, with **a Traditional 401K or Traditional IRA**, retirement contributions are made with *PRE-TAX INCOME*, so you pay taxes later in retirement when you withdraw the money. You are taxed depending on your post-retirement income bracket, which should be fairly low since you are not working anymore (usually 12%). This is often ideal for most high earning doctors because we want to REDUCE OUR TAXABLE INCOME during our peak career.

In a **Roth 401K or Roth-IRA,** retirement contributions are made with *AFTER-TAX INCOME* since you already pay taxes on your income when you get your paycheck (usually W2) so this allows the profit gains grow tax-free (*which is freaking awesome*). This is often ideal for low-earning jobs or optometrists during Residency.

Example: Let's use a main employer-sponsored 401K account (which has a max employee contribution of $19,000 for 2019). For example, Dr. Snow has an annual salary of $115,000 with an employer-sponsored 401K account, and has the choice to go the Traditional or Roth route, *which one does he chose?*

Since Dr. Snow is in significant high tax bracket now (Federal=24%), he wants as much deduction as possible to lower his taxable income. So, he would want to do *Traditional 401K* and contribute pre-tax dollars now. This will allow him to pay the taxes later when he retires. Assuming that when he retires at 65 years old and only has to withdraw less than $40,000 from his retirement accounts for living expenses, so essentially, he will only be taxed at 12%! (thus in one of the lowest tax brackets).

This is the **MOST tax-effective way for high-earning doctors.**

But for low earners like Optometry residents or students, Roth 401K or Roth IRA make way more sense because their income will eventually go up in the future so it is much better to take advantage of their low tax bracket now. *But when in doubt, the tie always goes to Roth.*

Why is the Roth IRA so Awesome?

All right, let's talk about the amazing and hidden powers of this tax-efficient retirement account. The Roth IRA is so complicated in its details that there is literally been a whole book written solely devoted to the topic. We are going to give you the basics of why we love the Roth IRA so much and why it should be a part of every high-earning professional portfolio.

So, as you know, anyone with earned income (regardless of 1099 or W2) can open a Roth IRA via Vanguard or Fidelity and can contribute $6,000 each year for 2019 (and another $6000 for your married babe if you want). The great thing about a Roth IRA is that you have access to a variety of great and cheap choices of mutual funds, unlike those automatically chosen within your 401K by your employer. Also, it is extremely easy to set up!

The one awesome thing is that since you contribute a Roth-IRA with after-tax money, the contributions can NEVER be taxed ever again (DUH, because you already paid taxes to Uncle Sam). Also, your capital gains (or how much your investment funds grow in profit) will also come out *TAX-FREE.* This is the principal reason why the Roth IRA is so freaking awesome because it doesn't have to pay the typical income tax upon withdrawal, like those in a traditional 401K or even the 15% long-term capital gain tax in a typical Taxable Brokerage investment.

Example: Dr. McLovin is one lazy 30-year-old bastard when it comes to retirement investment and only contributes $6000 each year to his Roth IRA out of his huge paycheck. If he is planning to retire at 65 years old and assuming an 8% growth each year, his total contribution (how much he put in) will only be $210,000 but his growth gains will be a **WHOPPING $906,612.** This allows Dr. McLovin to retire a millionaire (Total net worth of $1,116,612) by doing the bare minimum (see how little effort it takes to be rich??).

Okay, so let talk about the **tax implication**! Since it is in a Roth IRA, that $906,612 is all yours! Uncle Sam can't touch it anymore.

But if this was in a Traditional 401K, you will have to put taxes *BOTH on the contribution and gains*. Therefore, assuming you are at the lowest Tax Bracket of 15% in retirement, and you pull out all the money slowly over time, your overall tax bill on the total $1,116,612 within the traditional 401K, would be estimated *tax bill loss of $167,491 to Uncle Sam.*

What about Withdrawals on Contribution or Gains in a Roth IRA?

While you can withdraw the Roth IRA *contributions* at all time *WITHOUT penalty or taxes*, there are some strict rules of your GAINS, Profits WITHDRAWAL.

<u>5-year Rule:</u> You can only withdraw your gains *5 years after* you open your Roth IRA account. For example, if you made a Roth IRA contribution in February 2018 and assign it for 2017 Tax year (Remember you have up until April 2018 Tax Deadline to make any Roth contribution for 2017), you will have to wait until 1/1/2022 to withdraw any Roth IRA earning.

Similar to other retirement account, you still have to wait until they are <u>59 ½ years old to withdraw any gains</u> to avoid the **10% penalty.**

What are some Expectations to avoid the 10% Penalty for gain withdrawal?

1. Hardship periods such as disability and high medical expense.

2. Higher Education Schooling (can be applied to your spouse, or children/grandchildren).

1. Up to $10,000 per spouse, for a first-time home purchase (can be applied to your grandparents or children/grandchildren as long as it is their 1st home purchase).

Also, many doctors want to retire as early as 50 years old but cannot access their Trad-401K or IRAs until 59 ½, so a great strategy is to spend any tax-free Roth IRA contributions to fund their retirement from 50 to 59 ½ year old without the 10% penalty. Then after 59 ½ they can tap the fund in their traditional 401K funds.

Lastly, while we strongly do not recommend this route since *the funds in your Roth IRA should be only strictly reserved for retirement*, some investors can use their Roth IRA as a source for additional emergency funds in dire financial situation such as a life-saving medical operation.

The Back-Door Roth IRA

You might be asking, *"Wait Dat, most Doctors salary are way above the income $137,000 limit and cannot qualify for a Roth IRA! So why are we even talking about this?"*

You are absolutely correct!

To qualify for a Roth IRA, in 2019, you need to have a modified adjusted gross income of **under $137,000** (start to phase out contribution level at $122,000) for single individuals, and for married filing jointly, the max income is $203,000 (start to phase out contribution level at $193,000). So how do many high-earning professionals get around this??

There is a wonderful IRS loophole called the *BACKDOOR Roth IRA.* It is basically for the high earning professional whose income is above $137,000 and wants to open a Roth IRA. There are many online tutorials on how to do this, but you can basically open a Traditional IRA (ex: via Vanguard) and deposit the full $6,000 max amount. Then, the next day, you convert it to the Roth IRA. You simply repeat this each year.

Why is this even legal? Some financial advisors argued that it is just a way for the IRS to track their budget but Congress officially blessed the backdoor Roth IRA for everyone back in 2018.

The Roth IRA is a powerhouse when it comes to all these different tools and is a great way to diversify your retirement tax.

What is a Health Saving Account (HSA) aka "Stealth IRA"?

Alright, let's chat about the Ninja in the Room (Haha, I crack myself up) which is the Health Saving Account (HSA). If you are enrolled in a high-deductible health insurance plan, you can open an HSA either outside or via your employer. For 2019, the maximum contribution is **$3,500 for single individual and $7,000 for Family.**

Here are 5 great things about HSA:

1. Funded with Pre-tax dollars, basically a great tax deduction
2. You can use the funds at any time for any health-care expenses, without any tax paid or 10% penalty
3. There are no taxes on growth and you can also withdraw Tax-free for medical expenses
4. After age 65, you can withdraw from your HSA *without penalty after age 65 for anything at all*, but you just have to pay income tax rate. Thus acting as **"Another retirement account".**
5. You don't have to use all the funds by end of the year like a Flexible plan (FSA) or Health reimbursement (HRA). Also, the funds carry over after you leave your old job.

6. Able to use money contribution to invests in any mutual funds within the HSA account for maximum return.

The great thing about HSA is **TRIPLE TAX ADVANTAGED** if you use the money for medical expenses, which will be significantly needed, as you get older. In addition, HSA acts like an additional retirement vehicle to park your money efficiently from taxes, hence the name *"Stealth IRA"*.

Now that you are all educated about the crazy world of retirement accounts, let run through some real-life cases that will hopefully apply to your own situation.

Remember, our goal is to maximize the number of tax-efficient savings that a doctor can put away toward his retirement, depending on his or her tax situation. *Please feel free to refer to the Retirement account chart if needed.*

Doctor Case A:

Full time employed W2 doctor with an income of $120,000 with an employer-sponsored Traditional 401K plan with 5% match. Best way to max out retirement accounts:

1. Fund the Traditional 401K up to $19,000 with the 5% employer match.
2. Open a Traditional or Roth IRA (up to $6,000, max income limit is $137,000). *We recommend Roth IRA route due to tax-free growth.*
3. Dump the rest of his post-tax income paycheck into a Non-retirement Taxable brokerage account (No limit) with 15% long-term capital tax on any earnings.

This W2 doctor is in great shape and can contribute a significant amount of her income to retirement in a tax-efficient manner.

Doctor Case B:

Full time employed W2 doctor with an income of $110,000 but unfortunately her employer doesn't offer any Traditional 401K plan or any other SIMPLE IRA retirement plan. She does some casual fill-in at another optometry office and roughly has $10,000 in 1099 income. Best way to max out retirement accounts:

1. Open a traditional or Roth IRA (up to $6,000, max income limit is $137,000). In this case, either route is okay due to the doctor's income bracket. *But when in doubt, the tie goes to the Roth IRA.*

2. Open a SEP-IRA for her 1099 income, but she can only contribute *25% of her total 1099 income to the SEP IRA* (Ex: only $2500 can be contributed to her SEP IRA). She can deduct the 1099 contribution to SEP IRA when she files her end of year taxes.

3. Dump the rest of any post-tax income paycheck into a Non-retirement Taxable brokerage account (No limit) with 15% long-term capital tax on any earnings.

This W2 doctor has a *significantly more limited max contribution* to her retirement fund, compared to our Doctor A. It is great that she has some 1099 income on the side or else, the only thing that she can do is a Roth IRA.

Doctor B can also open a Solo-401K (rather than SEP-IRA) for her 1099 income as well, similar contribution but harder to set up. This will allow her to do a backdoor Roth-IRA if her income starts to rise past $137,000 limit in the future.

Doctor Case C:

Full time 1099 doctor with an income of $190,000, working for a private office where there is no employer-sponsored 401K or health benefits. She forms a S-Corp or LLC where she is both the employer/employee.

1. Open a Solo-401K for her 1099 income, but she can contribute $19,000 of her total 1099 income to the Solo-401K. She is also allowed to do an employer's match up of up to $37,000 but it cannot exceed 25% of her total income. Total: $47,500
2. She can deduct the 1099 contribution to Solo-401K when she files her end of year taxes
3. Open a Backdoor Roth IRA (up to $6,000, since max income limit is $137,000)
4. Dump the rest of any post-tax income paycheck into a Non-retirement Taxable brokerage account (No limit) with 15% long-term capital tax on any earnings.

Since this Doctor C is all 1099 income with a high income, she should open a solo 401K account even though it takes more work to set up. This will *allow her to do a backdoor Roth IRA.* Technically, she can do a SEP IRA (similar contribution to Solo 401K) but it will complicate her tax situation when she tries to open her backdoor Roth IRA due to the Pro-Rata rule.

What is the Pro-Rata Rule?

We won't go into much detail, but basically the IRS requires you to perform a calculation end of the year where they will treat all your existing IRAs (such as SEP, SIMPLE, Traditional IRAS) as ONE BIG IRA account. This can complicates thing when you try to do a backdoor Roth conversion. Your Roth IRA will be taxed on the *"pro-rata"* *percentage of all your total pre-tax IRA balances* to the total of all your IRA balances. Unless you are willingly to convert ALL IRAs accounts to your Roth IRA, and willingly pay the huge tax bill to Uncle Sam (Remember, with Roth, you pay taxes now to avoid the taxes due on any gains in the future). Afterward, you technically only have one Massive Roth-IRA, then you can do the backdoor Roth IRA.

In Summary, it is complicated as heck so DO NOT attempt the backdoor Roth IRA if you have existing other main IRAS like a SIMPLE or SEP IRA.

Doctor Case D:

Full time Private Practice Business Owner Incorporated as LLC or S-Corp, and pay himself a W2 salary of $150,000

1. Open an Employer-sponsored Traditional 401K for himself but must allow all his staff members to participate (Up to $19,000 contribution max) if desired. This usually have high yearly management fee.
2. Open a Backdoor Roth IRA (up to $6,000, since max income limit is 137K).
3. Dump the rest of any post-tax income paycheck into a Non-retirement Taxable brokerage account (No limit) with 15% long-term capital tax on any earnings.

As private practice owner, you have the option to either pay yourself a salary as a W2 employee of your corporation or pay yourself as 1099 income independent. Being 1099 income allows you to still open a SIMPLE-IRA or SEP-IRA but again would complicate you opening a backdoor Roth IRA. Since taxes get more complicated with owning a business, it is highly recommended that a practice owner works with a CPA tax accountant to see which retirement account is best for his business.

Pay yourself FIRST and Make it <u>AUTOMATIC</u>

Have you ever look at your friends who are always complaining about money and wonder how they truly handle their finances?

They are not; they are probably living paycheck to paycheck.

They probably have trouble paying their bill and don't know how much to budget each month. *They are definitely NOT saving much of anything for retirement.*

It doesn't even matter if you are making $50,000 or $120,000 income a year. It all comes down to how much you spend. A doctor making

$120,000 salary but spending $130,000 on booze and beer, brand new Tesla, fancy Louis Vuitton purses and "new" iPhone models has a negative net worth of $10,000 and *is poorer than the homeless dude down the street.*

You know that one hotshot doctor who drives that fancy Mercedes Benz and wears a $30,000 Rolex watch? Yup, I can almost guarantee that he is living paycheck to paycheck and swimming in debt. He will have to work much longer in his 70s years to maintain that lavish lifestyle, and will never be financially free.

This is how poor people stay poor!

They play the victim, make excuses and constantly chase after that perfect Instagram lifestyle. I hate to break to you, you ain't no Kim Kardashian!

We were reading this one article about how this one young self-entitled dumbass software engineer in Silicon Valley making over $150,000 a year and *struggling financially to stay afloat.* Then he goes on to write about he just needed to have his $6 mocha latte with his $15 avocado toast each morning and how he spends $25 a day on Lunch. Then he went on to justify his $4,000 rent for a one-bedroom apartment in San Francisco and how it was vital to his happiness and his social life. And oh, he just leases a brand new Tesla because all the cool Tech bros were driving it.

It was just numbingly ridiculous how someone who makes that much income is unable to be financially successful. Don't be like that dumbass.

Poor people get into this mindset of ***PAYING OTHER PEOPLE FIRST.***

THIS IS WRONG.

They pay the government their taxes first, they pay the credit companies first, they pay their car lease loan first, and then they might pay TicketMaster for that front-row concert tickets to see Beyoncé....

Then, the vicious cycle continues for 4 weeks until the end of the month when they are left with $20 in their checking account. Then they complain how they are unable to save! Do you know how Rich people get rich??? It is so simple.

THEY PAY THEMSELVES FIRST.

Before they even touch their paycheck, they automatically deposit a certain % amount toward their 401K retirement account, toward their student debt, or toward any saving accounts for their short-term financial goals. Then, they simply spend whatever is left over. This basically forces them to really prioritize what is actually NEEDED for their monthly budget, and help to eliminate WANTS.

I know you are thinking to yourself, I barely have enough to support all my expenses within my budget!

I am going to give you a shocking statistic right now. For a single individual living in San Francisco (one of the highest cost of living in the USA), to basically survive with bare essentials such as cheapest rent, basic groceries, medical insurance, basic necessities, etc., it is calculated that they only need $13,368 a year. *This equates to $1,114 a month for basic needs.* Sorry buddy, but basic needs don't include that Netflix subscription or pricey $1000 iPhone. Also, please keep in mind that this is for San Francisco CA, one of the most expensive cities in the USA.

So, there shouldn't be any excuse for an optometrist making a typical minimum salary of $100,000 a year to save for retirement or aggressively paying off their student debt. Remember:

PAY YOURSELF FIRST, your 65 years old self will be forever grateful.

You should always have enough money for the basic essentials on a doctor's salary. Anything extra above your budget, retirement, savings or student debt payments, then sure, goes ahead and enjoy it.

The final step is to MAKE IT AUTOMATIC.

Being financially successful should *require the most work initially* but once you set up all your investments and 401K accounts, it is basically on autopilot. Most retirement accounts or short-term saving accounts will have an automatic online deposit option that can promptly withdraw from one's checking account at the beginning of each month. The less you think about saving money, the easier that it is for you to pay yourself first.

In summary, we honestly hate the term 'retirement'. It invokes this idea of a lazy bum who is lying on a beach every single day and doesn't contribute anything to society. We save money and invest for one single reason, to be *financially free.* Free to do whatever your heart desires with having to worry about paying the bill. Being financially free allows us doctors after many years of schooling and hard work to pursue our true passions and dreams.

If your dream consists of you lying on the beach drinking Mai-Tais, then DUDE GO FOR IT. If you want to continue seeing patients, just imagine how much happier your day would be, knowing that you are helping patients simply because you enjoy it and not for a paycheck.

If you want to write the next great American Novel or start a side business or even a second career, you will now have the funds to take all the risk you want!

That is what investing for the future is all about, to achieve financial freedom

CHAPTER SEVEN: INVESTING 101 for Beginners: BY: Dat

"Investing should be more like watching paint dry or watching grass grow. If you want excitement, take $800 and go to Las Vegas."

- Paul Samuelson

I ran into a friend and colleague the other day at a coffee shop. She has been practicing for a few years in California, making a great income at a very-respectful private office. Super smart gal, I remember her graduating at the top 10 of her class back in Optometry school. We got to catching up and went on chatting about personal finance, in which I went on my usual spiel about mutual funds, tax-efficient retirement accounts, etc.

Within few minutes Tiffany interrupted me and stated that she wasn't investing or even funding her retirement accounts. I asked why not? Tiffany replied, *"Oh investing just seems really complicated so I just put everything in a saving account".*

This did not surprise me at all...

This was typical of most young doctors out of school. Personal finance simply is not taught in optometry school or anywhere in a formal classroom curriculum. I was in the same boat when I graduated from optometry school and got my first paycheck; I didn't even know what a Roth IRA freaking was and knew even less on how taxes actually worked! I actually felt so stupid for the first time in a long time. So, I can totally relate to how investing might seem intimidating.

When you hear investing, you conceptualize this image of a middle-aged white dude on Wall Street frantically yelling "BUY IT NOW! SELL IT NOW!" at the Dow-Jones ticker display. *Average, everyday investing is nothing like that.* Investing is actually quite boring and mundane, like watching grass grow.

The great thing about investing is that you can go as complex or as basic as you want. Even having a basic understanding of investing is enough to make you a successful investor! If you have the smarts to get through 4 hardcore years of optometry and memorize all those corneal dystrophies, *you can invest!*

With the online ease of passive low-cost index funds like Vanguard or Fidelity and advancement of robo-advisors such as Betterment or Wealthfront; the days of the high-fee actively-managed funds and financial advisors charging a **ridiculous 1-2% management fee is definitely coming to an end.** While, there will always be a small group of people who need professional help when it comes to their finances, most doctors can become do-it-yourself investors!

In the famous 2014 annual letter to his Berkshire stockholders, billionaire investor Warren Buffett stated if ever upon his death:

"My advice to the trustee [for my wife] could not be more simple: Put 10% of the cash in short-term government bonds and 90% in very low-cost S&P 500 index mutual fund. That's it"

Before we dive into the world of stocks and investing, we just want to give an **IMPORTANT DISCLAIMER!** This book is in NO WAY a massive in-depth investing textbook (our book would be over 10,000 pages long). Our goal for this chapter is simply to give you basic knowledge on how to get started, pitfalls to avoid, tips to maximize your earnings, and recommendations for investing resources!

Down the line, if you want to get more involved or complicated, there are many investing books out there. We are also going to be using Vanguard funds a lot in our examples, because we love their low-cost fee. Other brokerage companies include Fidelity, Charles Schwab or E-trade, and are just as good. Just in case you are wondering, sadly Vanguard is not paying us to promote their companies or financial products.

By the end of this chapter, you should be able to know:
- **Basic and Key Investment terms**
- **How to set up a Basic Asset Allocation within your portfolio**
- **How to Open up an investment Account**
- **How to Quickly assess a mutual fund**
- **How to Rebalance (if needed) with age**
- **Tools to help monitor your investment**
- **Additional tips and pitfall mistakes to avoid**

What is an Investment?

The Merriam Webster dictionary defines the word "investment" as the *outlay of money usually for income or profit: capital outlay.* In modern times, the word *investment* has been used, overused and many times, misused.

Take a look at the chart. Notice that amongst these items listed under "Investment," each one has the ability to *produce value,* whether it is through income, equity or perceived value by a fellow consumer.

Investment	Not an Investment
1) Stocks	1. Currencies like the Yen
2) Bonds	2. Cryptocurrency
3) Mutual Funds	3. Multi-Level Marketing
4) ETFs	(MLM)
5) Businesses	4. Your personal house
6) Real Estate	5. Cars and baseball cards
7) Hedge Funds	6. Appliances and
8) Private Equity	household items
9) Rare Material with High	7. The lottery/gambling
Demand relative to Supply	

While none of the items under the "Not an Investment" side of the chart have intrinsic value as we have defined above, remember that certain items can be used to make money (and subsequently lose money), such as crypto-currency or gambling. However, they do not qualify for our traditional definition of an investment. These items are based *mostly on speculation and chance,* rather than their ability to generate income.

Ok, let's start with some basic investing terminology so we can have a solid foundation and understand investing lingo.

What is a Stock?

Shares of ownership in a company sometimes referred to as stock equity. There are many different ways to own stock of a company or multiples companies like buying a simple S&P 500 index, where you can share in the profits (also losses) of a specific company like Apple. There are 2 basic way to own a stock.

(1) Individual Stock

Where you buy shares of a specific company like Amazon through a broker. It is often considered higher risk because you are placing all your money into a SINGLE company. So yes, there is a chance that the small company will be the next Apple, but it can also go bankrupt like Lehman Brothers (Remember the Recession/Housing Crash of 2008). For many investors, new and even the most experienced, we *DO NOT recommend individual stocks* (We explain why more in detail at the end of the chapter)

(2) Index Stock Fund

A stock can be purchased within a Stock Index or part of mutual fund and this is *generally the safest way to* own a stock. We always recommend low-cost, passive index funds such as Total stock index fund (tracks all the US stocks) or an S&P 500 Index fund (tracks the top 500 companies in USA). *The average Return for Stock Index is ~10%.*

What is the Difference between a Mutual Fund vs Index Fund vs Exchange-Traded Funds ETF?

1) Mutual Funds:

A large collection of money from multiple investors that is *actively controlled by* a fund manager, which they use to purchase different stock or bonds, along with other types of investment such as real estate. Mutual funds are great because they take away the decision-making stress of individual stocks and place this responsibility into the hands of an investment professional...but at a cost: *usually 0.50%-1.0%*, but sometimes as high as 2.5%

2) Index Fund:

Basically, the same thing as a mutual fund but managed by a computer, thus they are *passively controlled*, resulting in much lower costs. They essentially track and match the performance of any index such as healthcare, real estate, tech sectors etc. The most widely used index is the S&P 500 (*which tracks the performance of the 500 largest companies in US*). Passively managed index funds are great and highly recommended due to their extremely low-cost fee, *usually as low as 0.08% or 0% fee* like those from Fidelity

3) Exchange-Traded Funds (ETFs):

Identical to index funds which are passive and low-cost, but you have more options with specific indices, such as healthcare only. Also, you can sell/trade/buy ETFs at any time during market opening times, similar to an individual stock.

What is a Bond?

Basically, a sub-set of loans made to companies and the government, but is a part of a larger loan amount. Bonds can usually range in maturity (when it gets paid out) from 1 year to 25 years, in which the borrower (ex: US Government) agrees to pay back the loans to investors in full with interest, which is the gain. **Average Return for Bonds is ~2-3%.**

Bonds usually have very low return and are considered to be "safe." It serves one purpose, to *reduce volatility* within a portfolio during time of market lows. Again, similar to a Total Stock Index, we recommend doing a simple, low cost, passive *Total Bond Market index mutual fund.*

What is an Expense Ratio?

This is what the mutual or Index fund charges its investor for management per year, usually in the form of a percentage (or basis point). This includes the management (depending on how complex the assets in the funds are) and operating administrative fees. This is extremely important to know because it takes away from your net gain. *Remember that this is in ADDITION to a typical financial advising fee of 1-2% if you decide to hire a financial advisor.*

Example: An actively managed mutual fund can have an expense ratio of 1.80% (or 180 basis points) vs. a passively-managed index fund can have an expense ratio of 0.02% (or 2 basis point).

What is an Asset Allocation?

This is a breakdown of your overall investment portfolio. An asset refers to an investment type such as stock, bonds or other commodities like gold/silver.

Example: For a young investor in his 20-30s, his portfolio might be typically 90% stocks and 10% bonds. Stocks investments can come in many forms and might be further divided into index stock funds, emerging market stocks, international stocks etc. *We will go into more in asset allocation later.*

What are Asset Classes?

This is basically a group of investments that are similar to each other and have common trends in the market. The 2 major asset classes are stocks and bonds. Other less common asset classes can include money market, commodities (such as gold/silver), REITS (real estate investment trust). We will primarily focus on stocks and bonds in this book.

Remember that financial terms, just like eye anatomy, have their own language. So, having a solid grasp of these terms will help you be a more successful investor and increase the complication of your portfolio if desired.

How to do a proper Asset Allocation?

This might be the most important (and often most stressful) decision that an investor will make when it comes to his retirement account or other taxable investing account. A lot of investors often obsess over this step, but an asset allocation can be either complex or simple and still work perfectly. We advocate keeping it as simple as possible. Even the most successful investor can have his or her entire portfolio consisting of only 3-5 funds. Here are three basic steps to creating the perfect asset allocation game plan:

- (1) Select what % to invest in Stocks versus Bonds
- (2) Within your stock portion, choose which types of stock you want to invest in (mutual funds, index funds, individual stocks)
- (3) Adjust your asset allocation each year

Step 1) Selecting what % to invest in Stocks v. Bonds?

First of all, every investor is different depending on his or her personality and risk tolerance. The higher your risk tolerance, the more stocks you can handle in your portfolio.

Example: If you have $500,000 in investments/retirement account with 100% stock portfolio, then if you experience a 50% market loss (Similar to Recession/market crash of 2008-09), *can you stomach a loss of $250,000 while you wait 4-5 years for your funds to get back to baseline?* If not, lean toward more bonds allocation.

Secondly, look at when you actually need the money. For most investors, this is **when you are planning to retire.**

Most investments are considered long term (greater than 5 years) because this will allow the market to recover back from a crash and go back to a decent baseline. For example, it wasn't until 2012 that most investors were able to accumulate some of the funds that they lost during the 2008 crash.

For long term investing, *a good rule is as you approach retirement age; try to allocate a larger percentage of your portfolio towards MORE BONDS.* It would be a significant catastrophe to your finances if you are 64 years old and have a 100% stock portfolio, then a huge MARKET CRASH occurs! This would cause a loss of 50% in your 401K. This would force you to work *an additional 5 years* to allow the market to recuperate some of your losses. In general, when investing for decades on end, expect your portfolio to drop at least 20% during those times.

Once you are completely aware of all these factors, then you can choose an asset allocation that is right for you and allows you to sleep at night. Just make sure you STICK with it, through market crashes and gains!

As more Americans are living longer in retirement, a simple rule to determine how much stock to have in your portfolio is:

> **120 - Age = % of Stocks in Total Portfolio**

Example: A 30-year-old investor should have 90% stock + 10% bond mixture, while a 60-year-old investor should have 60% stock + 40% bond mixture since he is approaching retirement age.

Here is a Recommended Guide on the Stock to Bond Ratio you should have for your age range:

Age	Amount of Bonds	Amount of Stocks %
20-30	0 %	100%
30-40	10%	90%
40-50	20%	80%
50-60	30%	70%
> 60	40%	60%

To be honest, if you are a young investor in your 20s or early 30s, and you want to do a 100% stock portfolio, *that is perfectly okay!* I know plenty of young investors who have all stock portfolios because they want the highest return yield (for example, the Vanguard Total Stock Market Index Fund has a return of 10.5% over a 15-year course). As long as they understand their risk and can emotionally stick with their game plan even through a crash, then yes, their return will be significantly higher. It is acceptable for younger long-term investors to take more risk with stocks because they have a longer investing period to recoup any losses.

Which Bond Fund Should I choose?

You guess it! A simple, a low-cost passive Total Bond index fund such as the **Vanguard Total Bond Market Index Fund**.

This great index has a ridiculously low expense ratio (annual cost of the fund) of 0.15%. What is the annual gain of this bond over an average of 10 years? **Barely 3.5%!** Just enough to beat the inflation rate increase of 3-4% each year. As we told you, bonds are not meant to create significant wealth, but they are simply there to create stability in one's portfolio.

There are other types of bonds out there ranging from TIPPS (Treasury Inflation Protected Securities), high-yield corporate bonds or government bonds. As you become a more experienced investor, you might want to dabble more into the intricacies of bond allocation. For now, keep it simple and easy and chose a Total Bond Index Fund that has all types of bonds within it.

Step 2) Within my stock portfolio portion, which Specific Types of Stock do I invest in?

Domestic US Stocks should be main foundation of any typical portfolio (Close to 75%). The US economy is the strongest market in the world compared to other international countries. So, this is going to be your moneymaker right here! The US Total Stock Index has some years that have seen as high as a 33% gain (2013) but also, some years as low as -37% loss (2008 crash). Typically, US stocks over the course of 15 years have an average return of **10.5%,** which isn't too shabby!

There are many different types of stocks out there. Below are summaries of each class for you to get a general idea.

US Domestic Stocks vs. International Stocks

US domestic stock funds invest only in US-based companies like Amazon or General Electric, while international stock funds invest in companies from Chinese Alibaba ("The Amazon of China") or European Volkswagen.

The whole idea of having a *small 25% portion of your stock portfolio in International stocks* is to diversify your portfolio. So, if the US economy isn't doing so hot, then you stabilize your returns with other international market.

The question is do you really need international stocks in your portfolio? ABSOLUTELY NOT! While some investment experts recommend 25% of your stock portfolio to consist of international stock, many financial analysts argue that a lot of US-based companies do business in international market (ex: Apple sells iPhones in China) thus giving you *indirect international exposure.* So basically, you do not need a 25% portion devoted to international stock unless you want to.

Large Cap vs. Medium Cap vs. Small Cap Stocks

The capitalization size of a fund tells you if they are investing in a large or small company. Large-cap funds invest in $10-100 billion or greater giant businesses like Apple and Chevron, while mid-cap fund invest in $2-10 billion companies like Guess and Urban outfitters. Lastly, small-cap funds invest in $250 million to 2 billion companies such as Spectrum pharmaceuticals or Lithia Motors. Many of these smaller companies are unknown to the general public.

As a general rule, large-cap mutual funds will focus on the largest US companies and thus, *will be the safest and more stable returns* but they *might not be the largest returns.* Small-cap mutual funds focus on the

103

smaller but faster-growing companies, which result in higher risk but *can have the highest returns.* Mid-cap is the best of both worlds.

Now that you have a handle on the basic types of stocks, let's explore stock allocation.

Example: Assuming that a young 30-year-old doctor investor wants to go for a 100% stock portfolio (ignoring the bond portion for now), what would the reasonable stock fund profile be?

Let's use Vanguard mutual funds for example. These four passive-index and low-cost stock fund types that should be the CORE of your portfolio:

1. **Vanguard Total Stock Market Index Fund (VTSMX):** Tracks the performance of all stocks in the USA.
2. **Vanguard S&P 500 Stock Index Fund (VFINX):** Tracks the performance of the top 500 (mainly large-cap) stocks in the USA.
3. **Vanguard Small Cap Stock Index Fund (VSMAX):** Tracks the performance of all small-cap stocks in the USA.
4. **Vanguard Total International Stock Index Fund (VGTSX):** Tracks the performance of all international stocks outside of USA.

Here are **4 great and simple portfolio examples** that are ideal for any investor, either beginner or expert.

	Portfolio #1	Portfolio #2	Portfolio #3	Portfolio #4
25% of total Stock	Vanguard Total Stock Market Index Fund	Vanguard S&P 500 Stock Index Fund	Vanguard Total Stock Market Index Fund	Vanguard Total Stock Market Index Fund
25% of total Stock	Vanguard S&P 500 Stock Index Fund			------Or------ Vanguard S&P 500 Stock Index Fund
25% of total Stock	Vanguard Small Cap Stock Index Fund	Vanguard Small Cap Stock Index Fund		
25% of total Stock	Vanguard Total International Stock Index Fund	Vanguard Total International Stock Index Fund	Vanguard Total International Stock Index Fund	

> **+** Plus **Vanguard Total Bond Market Index Fund**
> (Whatever % of total portfolio that you devote to Bond)

The goal of each portfolio is to diversify your asset allocation and have exposure in each field.

Portfolio #1 has a straight strategy of allocating 25% to each major fund, thus giving us equal exposure. Both the Total Stock Market and the S&P 500 funds are similar to each other but each or both funds should be *the main core of any portfolio.*

Portfolio #2 has half of its allocation in S&P 500 funds, which is mainly large-cap, and some mid-cap companies, thus it is wise to have exposure to a small-cap stock fund, *basically tilting your portfolio to smaller companies.*

Portfolio #3 essentially combine S&P 500 and Small-Cap Index into one single Total Stock Market fund, basically giving us exposure to all three tiers of stock (Large, mid, small).

So, you might ask why the heck does **Portfolio #4** exist when there is no international exposure?   Once again, remember that indirect exposure to international markets exists in the US stock market.

Asset allocation is as much an art as it is a science. All four portfolios have their own merits and strengths, therefore offering great diversification. Many investors want to keep it as simple as possible with the lowest number of funds, so *usually portfolio #3 or #4 will be appealing to them.* You will be successful in investing with either allocation and you can always increase the complexity of your portfolio as you expand your financial knowledge.

Step 3) Rebalance your asset allocation each year

Let's assume for today, you've chosen to invest 70% in stock mutual funds and 30% in bonds at the beginning of 2019. Then, as the prices of stocks and bonds change with the market toward the end of the year, your portfolio might result in 75% in stocks and 25% in bonds. Therefore, rebalancing is *simply correcting the imbalance* by returning to the original 70% to 30% allocation.

A lot of investors rebalance more frequently (like every month, which is extremely excessive) or when their portfolio reaches a certain threshold like 40% stock. We recommend keeping it simple, so *rebalancing ONCE A YEAR* is good enough.

Many 401K or IRA accounts will have options to allow investors to set the % of their mutual funds to the desired stock and bond asset allocation, thus making rebalancing easy and done within 5 minutes.

Obviously, the more asset classes you have (like commodities, REITS) or multiple IRA accounts, then the more difficult it will be.

What are other Additional Asset Classes?

Let's quickly go over some of the other types of investment that you can include within your portfolio. Do you need any of these Asset classes to be successful? *Absolutely NOT!*

As you become more experienced with your investing knowledge and want to diversify into other fields, then feel free to. We usually recommend **only allocating 5-10% of your total portfolio** to these smaller investments:

1) Emerging Markets Mutual Funds:
These stock mutual funds focus on companies that are in developing or emerging countries like Brazil and surprisingly China. These countries are not under-developed but not yet fully developed; So they tend to have a much faster rate of growth (thus, higher returns) compared to developed US Domestic companies' stock. **The catch? - They are very volatile with extreme losses or gains as much as 50-90% within a few months** *(I am talking to you Latin America!)*. A lot of investors like to have 10% max devoted to emerging markets funds to help balance risk and reward.

2) REITs (Real Estate Investment Trusts) Mutual funds:

If you have an interest in real estate but don't have the necessary funds (or interest) to buy properties, then REITs are a great way to get your hands dirty without taking on the risk of being a landlord.

REITS basically invest in companies that buy up or invest in all different types of real estate properties, from commercial to personal. Again, REITS are not necessary, but offer another way to diversify your portfolio. They are *extremely tax inefficient* due to constant gains and dividend payout, so these should strictly be in a tax-deferred retirement account like an IRA or 401K.

4) Commodities Mutual Fund:

These funds basically invest in items like agricultural goods, natural resources and/or precious metal such as gold and silver. They have an *extremely low rate of return* and are considered a poor long-term investment. **We recommend NOT investing in simple commodities like gold or weed since they are an awful investment and don't produce anything** (unlike stock in a company).

From 1836 to 2011 (accounting for inflation), the long-term return on gold is a *ridiculously low 1.1%*. If you want to invest in precious metal, do so in a commodity mutual fund or better yet, invest in the stock of a company that uses commodities like Starbucks (Coffee) or Exxon Mobil (gas). Many companies use commodities as their material, thus giving you an indirect exposure to commodities.

What about Individual Stocks?

You might be asking yourself right now. What about individual stocks? Investing in a specific company like Apple or Tesla is basically like *gambling to some degree* and often requires extensive research into the financial background, earning reports and future analysis of that company.

To be a successful individual stock investor, you have to be able to critically assess the value of how much the company is worth and keep up with current events and quarterly earnings of that company. This often causes significant stress for beginning investors. But if one can correctly invest in the right company, like the next Google or Apple, then obviously the earning potential investment will be significantly great!

Over time, as you become a more experienced investors and want to dabble in individual stocks, by all means, do! It is a great way to diversify your portfolio and increase earning potential. However, with all of that being said, investing in individual stocks is not for everyone and it is NOT EVEN NEEDED to be a successful investor. For the majority of investors, we recommend sticking with *low-cost, passive stock index funds as the core of your portfolio* and you will do just great!

How to Quickly assess a Mutual or Index Fund?

You are probably looking at your 401K list of mutual fund choices and getting confused with all the numbers. We are going to teach you how to *quickly evaluate a mutual fund in less than 60 seconds* with a few simple steps:

1) Find all the funds that are similar to your asset allocation:

I know we have been using Vanguard as our prime example, but many other big brokerage firms like Fidelity will have similar funds with similar names. It is quite common for some 401K plans to have mutual funds like a total market stock index fund, so you need to find something similar.

2) Enter the Fund's Ticker symbol:

We recommend Morningstar.com or YahooFinance.com. This will allow us to see what type of assets the fund actually invests in, such as Stock vs Bond, Large vs Small cap companies or Foreign vs Domestic bonds/stocks, etc

Example: Vanguard Mid-Cap Growth Index fund with the ticker symbol VMGRX has the majority of its holding in mid-cap US stock.

3) Select NO-LOAD funds only:

Make sure that there is no additional fee charged (*sometime up to 5%*) required for you to buy the fund. Usually this fee can be charged prior to purchase (FRONT-Loaded) or after a certain time (BACK-loaded). If you look at the "load option" on any mutual fund on Morningstar, the no-load fund will show "none"

4) Look for the lowest Expense-ratio ("Cost of fund"):

This is probably the most important factor when picking a fund and will cost significant earnings in the long run if too high. Most low-cost passive index funds will be significantly less than 0.50% (or expense ratio of 50) but many are even as low as 0.05%.

Avoid actively managed mutual funds that can have a much higher expense ratio. If you have no other choices on your 401K list, the most cost we would *accept is less than 1%.*

5) Past Performance of Earnings:

While past performance does NOT indicate future performance of the funds, it does offer us to have some insight in the pattern of the fund itself. Just take a look at its performance after the 1st year, 3rd year and 10th year to get a sense of its average gains for short-term and long-term.

Example: As of 2018, the Vanguard Total Stock Market Index (VTSMX) has a performance of 1 year= 21.05%, 3 years=10.96% and 10 years= 8.60%. Don't get too excited with the 21.05% performance gain because it is *definitely not the norm* - 2017 was a really great year! An average return of 8.60% (over a course of 10 years) is a more realistic return long-term during an investor's lifetime.

You can definitely dive into the complicated details of each fund as you build your investing knowledge, but this basic knowledge is more than enough to quickly evaluate the fund.

What about Target-Date Retirement Funds?

At this point, if you are still confused and thinking to yourself *"I hate all this financial nonsense, I went to a school to be a doctor and I don't care about what an expense ratio is!"* – That is completely okay.

While we promote do-it-yourself investing, we are aware that not everyone will have the same financial interests, especially doctors. Just by reading this book, you already have the necessary background to understand the basics.

So, what is the solution if you want to avoid all these headaches? *Choosing a Target Date Retirement Mutual Fund.* This is basically the One Ring to rule them all (and we have officially met our nerdy Lord of the Rings reference quota). Most 401K or retirement plans will offer a Target-Date Fund, which allows you to choose a fund that closely matches when you want to retire.

Example: If I am 30 years old (as of 2019) and want to retire at 65 years old or around year 2049, ideally, I want to choose a Mutual fund with a target date of 2050 such as *Vanguard Target Retirement 2050 Fund.*

Target date retirement funds will automatically rebalance your asset of stocks and bonds each year, with more emphasis of bonds as you approaching retirement age. But if you are in your 30s, the fund will be more weighed on stocks which have a higher return but more risk.

You also have little flexibility in selection as well. If you want to be more aggressive with stocks, then just select a later target date retirement fund like Vanguard Target Retirement 2065, rather than

Vanguard Target Retirement 2050 Fund. There isn't going to be a red alarm going off in your 401K selections if you didn't select the fund date that matches up with your retirement date. The only downside is you don't have as much control with funds inside the plan and most target date retirement funds will be **slightly more expensive** than a S&P 500 Index fund.

For a new investor, target date retirement funds are a great choice and much easier to start with! Once you want to be more in charge of your investments, you can always change your investment options later.

What about Robo-Advisors?

Well, it is definitely not some Japanese Mecha-Unit that is going to doing all your stock picks for you. Wait, I guess in a sense it is?

Robo-advisors are basically online, automated portfolio services that use computer algorithms to choose the appropriate investments (stock vs bonds) based on your risk tolerance and time horizon. It also rebalances your assets each year as well. Thus, because it doesn't require an actual person or team of financial advisors/analyst, so the fee is much lower usually in the *range of 0.25% to 0.50%,* compared to a human financial advisor charging 1-2%. Therefore, it is a great way to get started.

Robo-advisor companies like **Betterment and Wealthfront** have become amazingly popular with the younger millennial investors. Why? To be honest it makes investing fun again. It engages the investor by making the investing process extremely user-friendly and easy; also, it tracks performance process each year with pretty graphs and charts.

The question is do you really need it? Again, while we advocate for do-it-yourself investing, we understand that some individuals require more handholding or don't want to deal with the headaches of selecting all these funds themselves, so Robo-Advisors are great for them! But *to be frank, Robo-Advisor basically does the same as **a simple low-cost target-date retirement mutual fund.*** This includes rebalancing the portfolio and stock to bonds selection, but without all the shiny lights and bells. But hey, if you don't mind paying that extra 0.25-0.50% fee, then go for it!

How to Monitor Your Investments and Track your performances?

The final step of any investing game plan is to track your investment and performances. You don't have to be all crazy about it and check it each day. But it *is recommended that you check it* at *least once a month*. It is easy to set an investment plan in motion like choosing a target date retirement or passive stock index fund, and then forget about it.

It is important to keep track of your finances. Also, it is really fun to see your investments grow and your student debt shrink with each passing month! We like to imagine each invested dollar as hundreds of tiny little workers, grinding 24/7 to earn us more income while we sleep.

Personal Capital (Website + mobile application) is a free app that basically links all your bank accounts, investment brokerage accounts, retirement accounts and your student loan account.

Then, it combines them all into an amazing dashboard where you can see all your asset allocations and what your true ratio of stocks to bonds are, your total net worth (*don't be too sad if it is negative due to your massive student debt*), total fee paid in mutual funds, etc.

Also, it offers a free retirement planner to let you know if you are on track for retirement or not and actually give you some insights and advice on whether your financial plan is working for you. Did we also mention that it is free?!

If you want to do it the old-fashioned way, a simple Microsoft excel
sheet to track your earnings is fine and dandy.

Summary: Tips and Advice

Congratulations! You finally made it to the end of this extremely long
chapter! Take a deep breath. You now understand all the basics of
Investing 101. Piece of cake compared to learning all the neural-
pathway of the trigeminal nerve, huh?

You probably absorbed all the financial knowledge that most of the
society takes years to even comprehend. Just by getting these basics,
you are ready to be a real player in the stock market.

When we were writing this investing chapter, we had two goals in
mind: Keep it simple and fun to understand, and talk about investing
pitfalls for young doctors to avoid.

Building wealth is a slow and boring process and requires time and
basic hard work (with hopefully minimal sacrifice), rather than
financial genius. Young doctors often are too impatient when it comes
to wealth building and this can lead to rash decisions like get-rich
schemes.

We don't blame you, you sacrificed and waited through 8 years of
undergraduate and optometry school and you want to be rich ASAP.
But hey, slow down, relax and take one step at a time. When you are
desperate and greedy, there will always be some form of Ponzi
scheme, Bitcoin mania, late night infomercial or multi-level marketing
scheme to prey on you.

There is a famous article by Dr. James Dahl MD titled *"6 Reasons why
Doctors get scammed"*. The article basically explains why many
doctors ended up broke because they consider themselves too busy or
too cocky to learn the basics of finances. This, coupled with no formal

education in personal finance and investing, *is a perfect storm waiting to happen.*

Many financial and insurance salesmen (sometime masked as advisors) will prey on the trusting nature of doctors. We as doctors, like to believe that any "financial professional" or "specialist" must always be correct and have our best interest at heart, similar to the way we treat our own patients. But the truth is - there is no Hippocratic oath for financial advisors.

Even the so-called "Fiduciary-certified" financial advisors will still have some form of bias, even if it's unconscious. Our best defense as doctors is to be educated and learn *how to take any given financial advice given with a grain of salt.*

Heck, I want you to take what you read today and question the hell out of everything we are teaching you. It will make you into a better investor and a better student.

Trust but verify, as you do everything else in life.

The Optometrist's Guide to Financial
Freedom

CHAPTER EIGHT: Pay off Debt vs. Investing: "What Should I do First?" BY: Dat

"Whatever interest rate you have — it might be a student loan with a 7 percent interest rate — if you pay off that loan, you're making 7 percent. That's your immediate return, which is a lot safer than trying to pick a stock or trying to pick real estate, or whatever it may be,"

-Mark Cuban

Personal finance is called *personal* for a reason; it is just as much a science as it is an art (similar to prescribing glasses). But seriously, this is probably *one of the most difficult decisions* that a lot of doctor investors will face and has starved me of sleep a lot - simply deciding which financial goal to attack first.

There are a lot of financial gurus that have come up with generic and quite frankly strict lists of "baby steps" that are supposed to cater to everyone. This is virtually impossible to do because everyone's situation is completely different and varies in complication.

A new graduate with massive student loans and high-interest credit card debt will have different priorities from a seasoned OD who is nearing retirement. We hope this chapter offers a guideline to help you analyze each of your financial goals and help you prioritize them in ways that cater to your own situation; most importantly, your own attitude toward debt and goals.

First thing to think about: think in **terms of goals.** List out what your personal goals related to finance are.

Do you want to pay off your student debt in 1-5 years or are you okay to have it for 10 years? Do you want to buy a home in a few years or are you okay to rent for a while? Do you want to open a private practice soon? Do you want to start a family sooner than later? Do you want to retire much earlier than the standard 65-year-old? Do you want to help take care of your elderly parents?

Now that you have given it some thought. List your goals here:

1) _____

2) _____

3) _____

4) _____

5) _____

Have more goals? – Grab another sheet of paper!

Everyone's goals are different, but many doctors should have these few common general financials goals:

1. **Have an emergency fund (3-6 months)**
2. **Pay off high interest consumer debt and/or non-mortgage debt (like student loans)**
3. **Save for retirement**
4. **Buy a house (save for a down payment)**
5. **Save for a private practice (if applicable)**
6. **Save for children's college education (if applicable)**

7. **Pay off the house mortgage**
8. **Give generously and live the life you want**

First, *your financial goals should be motivating and emotional;* they should be why you get up each morning to drive that one-hour commute to work or professionally deal with that ridiculous rude patient yelling at your front desk staff. This is why you can do the same *"One or two, which is clearer"* question day after day, year after year. No millionaire's goal is to simply have a million dollars in their bank account; it is what they plan to do with it that sparks joy in their lives.

The second thing is to **multi-task different priorities!** We do realize the power of intense focus and the behavioral aspect in putting all your concentration into one financial goal, such as aggressively paying off your student loans or saving up for a down payment on a house. But just as you were able to balance studying for both your binocular vision and ocular disease finals back in school, you should be able to multitask your financial goals.

The idea of an optometrist deferring his retirement fund by 5 or even 10 years while paying off student loans is *RIDICULOUS* when it comes to the power of compounding. Also, if your employer offers a 6% match to your 401k or IRA, contribute at least to that amount. That is *free money* that you are leaving on the table. Any company match is considered a part of your salary.

Third, **assess your own risk tolerance and attitude toward debt.** If you are not a risk-taker, then focus more on paying off debt vs. investing for retirement. If you do not mind leveraging on some debt, then focus more on investing for retirement.

If you look at the math, a typical student loan costing 6.8% interest (or even 2.9% if refinanced) might not seem as exciting as your S&P 500 index mutual fund stock portfolio gaining 11% yearly. But investing in your stock portfolio carries significant risk compared to a guaranteed "return" of 6.8% if you pay off your student loans. Your ability to assess your own risk attitude is an important part of your personality as an investor.

"Dat and Aaron! Argh, Can You Just Tell Me Where to Start?"

Here is a **"Guideline" list of financial steps** (as of 2019) that we hope will get you started, but should be adjusted to your own personal situation:

1. Establish an **Emergency Fund of 3-6months expenses (Not income).**
2. **Contribute to any main workplace tax-protected** retirement (Ex: 401K, SEP/SIMPLE IRA) funds *up to employer's match.*
3. **Pay off any high-interest debt (greater than 8%)** such as credit card debt and car lease loan.
4. **Invest in tax-protected retirement accounts (*10% minimum, and ideally 20-25%* once you are done with all non-mortgage debt)**
   a. Assuming $100,000 salary, you should be able to fund 5% toward your Roth-IRA at least and work toward funding another 5% to your workplace 401K or other major IRA like SEP/SIMPLE.
5. **Aggressively pay off all non-mortgage debt between 5-8%.** This should include most of your student loans of 6.8%
   a. Even if you refinanced your student loans to a lower rate of ~2.9%, you should still consider paying off your large student debt at this step despite the low interest rate.
6. **Fully max out ALL tax-deferred retirement accounts** such as you 401K/SEP/SIMPLE IRA (Ex: $19,000 for 401K) and Roth-IRA (or back door Roth IRA $6000). Try to have a goal of **20-25%** of your income toward retirement.

7. **Invest in a Health-Saving Account** (HSA: Up to $3,500 Single, $7,000 Family) if you have a high deductible medical plan.
8. **Invest in a Taxable account (long-term capital gain tax of ~15%: No Limits)** with mutual funds or CD/Bonds for other short-term financial goals (<5 years).
   a. Such as saving for a down payment on house (if applicable to your situation, with *a goal of 20% down home payment*).
9. **Save for your kid's college fund (if applicable)** by investing in other tax-deferred accounts such as Education Saving Account (ESA: $2,000 Limit with factor in income limit) or State 529s plan ($14,000 Limit to avoid tax).
10. **Pay off loans with after tax of 3-5%,** which includes most house mortgages or private practice business loans (at the time of writing this book).
11. **Pay off low-interest loans <3%.**
12. **Invest even more in Taxable Accounts** (such as mutual stock funds) or **real estate rental properties investment.**
13. **Live the life you work hard for; spend the money you earned and give generously.**

We do advise a lot of our doctor investors to *NOT carry any debt (including the house mortgage) into retirement* since losing the safety net of your job will cause significant financial risk.

But again, remember this is just a guideline! So, it is okay if you decide to place all your focus on aggressively paying off your student loans because you simply hate debt. Sometimes, it is okay to focus more on retirement or saving for a house down payment. Some years later, your goals might change and you want to aggressively attack your student debt. While other years, you want to invest more for retirement.

Just get create a game plan and get started!

CHAPTER NINE:"How Do I Accumulate Short Term Wealth? BY: Dat

"Setting goals is the first step in turning the invisible into the visible."
                                                        -Tony Robbins

For the majority of this book, we went in great depth on how to strategically invest our hard-earned money for the long term; Money that we are not supposed to touch until retirement. But so many of our readers ask the same question:

"How do I save money for the short-term to accomplish financial goals like saving for a down payment? A vehicle purchase? An engagement ring for my sweetheart? Or a rental property purchase?"

Everyone has different financial goals in life that are beyond just amassing money to be financially free.

Typically, most Americans put any extra cash needed in a standard savings accounts like your local Bank of America or Credit Union, where **the annual return is extremely low (~0.02%).** Shocking right? Especially when you consider annual inflation of 3-4% - you basically lose the purchasing power of the dollar with each passing year.

Therefore, short-term investment strategies are so vital in our financial plan. **So, what is considered a short-term investment?**

As a general rule, we will define a short-term investment as anything that will be spent in *5 years or less.* The quicker you need the cash, the less risk you will need to take.

So, you might be asking.... **Why 5 years?** Studies show that that on an average, it takes about 5 years for the stock market to recuperate some of its losses and go back to baseline (or Zero) after a bear market period or significant market correction.

Is it a guarantee that the market will recover to baseline after a crash? **NO.** If you look at the 1930s, there was a rather significant market crash (called the Great Depression) that even after 5 years still saw a loss of 60.9%. Fortunately, this scenario rarely occurs, however it does give us a glimpse of the inherent risk of the stock market.

What are 5 short-term investing vehicles?

1) Online High Yield Savings Account (Gain= 2.1 to 2.4%)
Still nothing to be excited about, Online High Yield Saving Accounts provide a better interest rate than 0.02% that you are getting from your bank and you are able to withdraw at any time. Also, they are still FDIC-insured, which means that the US government guarantees no losses of your funds. This is usually the most flexible and safest way to save for the short-term.

2) Certificate of Deposit a.k.a. "CD" (Gain= 1 to 2.5%)

With a CD, you agree to leave your money in the bank for a set amount of time (ranging from a few months to 5-20 years). *The longer the term, the higher the rate of return.* There is a penalty charged if you decide to withdraw prior to the maturation term, so it is critical that you select the correct timeframe. While it still doesn't beat inflation, it is FDIC insured.

3) Short Term Bond Index (Gain= 1 to 4%)

You can invest with Vanguard for short or intermediate bonds, in either US government or Corporate. Government bonds will be more secure but will pay less compared to corporate bonds. Bonds for the most part are considered a safe investment but they are not FDIC-insured. We would recommend a total bond index fund.

4) Municipal Bonds (Gain= 2 to 5% after tax)

Municipal bonds are when you lend money to a state or local government, and they pay you back with a specific interest. The one great thing about muni bonds are that there are *no taxes on the gain* and is great for high-earning professional like us. Like bonds, you can withdraw anytime without penalty.

5) Lending Club (Gain= 5-7%)

Lending clubs are basically peer-to-peer lending platforms that allow investors to give loans to individuals or smaller businesses. Loans are usually set for 3-5 years. It is very easy to invest and have a diversified lending loan portfolio for a higher return, but you run the risk for default loans made, plus it is difficult to liquefy the non-FDIC funds into cash if needed.

Why NOT just take the risk and do Mutual Funds mixing Stocks and Bonds?

This is often a great debate between investors. Why not take the risk and put some of those short-term needed capital into the stock mutual funds and get a higher return like 10%? It is difficult as an investor seeing the market rises 25% in one year (example: 2017) and looking at your puny little high-yield saving account earning a whopping return of 1.3%. However, with everything come with risks.

For example, if you were to invest $50,000 in stock mutual funds for a house down payment in 2007 (before the 2008 market crash) and hopefully withdraw it by 2010 for a future house purchase. *You would have lost close to 50% by end of 2009*, ending up with $25,000. This would force you to leave your money in for another 3 more years to get to baseline, *thus delaying your house purchase.*

Therefore, the general guideline is to avoid investing in the stock market if you need the money in **5 years or less**. It gives you time for your funds to get back to baseline and recover in the worst-case situation.

What about using the Roth IRA for short-term investing?

I know what you are probably thinking! *"Whoa! Dat and Aaron, you told me that retirement accounts are for retirement and not to pull out at any cost."* **You are absolutely right.** For the majority of investors, we never recommend touching your Roth IRA for anything except for retirement. It is an amazing tax-efficient account with tax-free growth.

But as mentioned in the previous chapter on retirement, the one cool thing about the Roth IRA is that you can withdraw the contributions (post-tax money you put in each year, up to $6,000 in 2019 at ANYTIME and WITHOUT any penalty or taxes, mainly because you pay taxes on the incoming Roth IRA funds already). However, you cannot pull out the gains without penalty until you are 59 ½ years old.

Some investors fully fund their 401K and devote it to retirement, and use their Roth IRA contributions as a way for short-term financial goals like saving for a house down payment. *Just realize that you are losing that retirement money forever*, along with any tax-free compounding growth as well. **Again, we do NOT advise using your Roth IRA as a way for short-term goals,** but it is another option of investing if you are aware of the risks and consequences.

Short-term investing is an important tool that we need to have in our portfolio, because it allows us to accomplish many of our financial goals throughout our lives. While saving for retirement is an important aspect in personal finance, it is money that you cannot touch until you are much older.

You work hard day after day, sometimes even 6 or 7 days a week, so it is just as important to be able to enjoy the short-term joy of your money as well.

The Optometrist's Guide to Financial Freedom

CHAPTER TEN: Practice Ownership- Buying and Thriving BY: Aaron

"You are the master of your destiny. You can influence, direct and control your own environment. You can make your life what you want it to be."

-Napoleon Hill

Optometry presents itself as a unique health care profession, in that nearly all practitioners have the opportunity to stake ownership in a practice. Practice ownership enables an individual to take full charge of their clinical identity and destiny.

Practice ownership, based on elementary economics, in theory will always *give more income as opposed to being employed.* However, the road to this higher income path is not necessarily smooth.

Owning a practice requires much more than the skillset you acquire in optometry school. In fact, most skills needed to run a successful practice simply come with experience and mistakes. Even if you decide to get an MBA under your belt, you will soon find that business ownership is not nearly as cut and dry as seeing patients.

If you find yourself entertaining the possibility of practice ownership, make sure you can answer these **five questions** definitively:

1) Can you take Multiple Responsibilities?

You're no longer just a doctor when you own a practice. Seeing patients becomes second nature as you juggle being an administrator, employer, marketer and accountant all at once.

2) Can You Make Tough Interpersonal Decisions?

With ownership, you're now responsible not only for yourself, but your staff and associate doctors. The responsibilities of hiring and firing fall on you.

3) Can you Stomach Periods of Negativity and Utilize the Experience for Future Growth?

No one said owning a great business was smooth sailing. Are you ready for periods of negative cash flow? Can you handle the idea of a pay cut if the money isn't coming in?

4) Can you take Ownership of Everything?

No more blaming others. You are the boss. Every mistake, whether it be your own or your employees', will fall on you. Do you have the character to own up in order to make your business even better?

5) Can You Eat It?

Not literally, but sometimes it may feel literal. If you want to truly succeed, you will need to embrace the long hours, extra work and be the brunt of everyone's frustration.

Ok, so you read through the five questions and you are ready to become a practice owner, without a shadow of doubt. You're sick of just being that 9-5 associate position making that middle-class salary. You want something more. You cling to that desire to create a legacy of your own.

Fantastic, let's go through some basics that will help you on your journey.

Business Basics - Cash Flow, Profit/Loss, Balance Sheets, etc.

This next section will cover the absolute basics that are needed to understand how a business runs and how to run a business successfully. We could write pages upon pages, book upon book explaining how a business works and how to run it. In fact, whole institutions exist with the sole goal of educating individuals about running businesses. However, the goal of this chapter is to simply provide you the *absolute essentials that are necessary* to understand for you to run a financially successful optometric business. There will be plenty of terms and equations. If the information appears overwhelming, don't worry! Focus on the concepts rather than the mathematical details.

Assets and Liabilities

The first key concept to understand in practice management is the idea of *assets* and *liabilities*, and how the fluctuation of each of these represents your total *equity*.

Assets represent everything that *adds value to a business* including available cash, equipment, inventory, patient fees, and accounts receivable. Liabilities represent everything that *negates value or cash* from a business including loan payments, rent/mortgage, monthly fees and depreciation.

In order to understand how much equity a given practice has, we use what is colloquially referred to as the **Accountant's Formula:**

> **Equity = Assets – Liabilities**

The accountant's formula is the basis for all bookkeeping and accounting of a practice.

Cash Flow

Cash flow, sometimes referred to as free cash flow, is a vital number that tells how financially healthy a practice is. A practice could be seeing over 40 patients a day and have negative cash flow, thus causing a loss of profit and subsequently lost income, if ran poorly. On the flipside, a practice could see 5 patients a day and generate positive cash flow if ran efficiently.

Cash flow is defined as cash a given business produces through its operation (aka *operating cash flow*) minus the funds expended on the business's assets. Thus, our cash flow equation is:

Free cash flow = Operating Cash Flow - Asset Expenditure

Let's break this down a little further. *Operating cash flow* refers to money the practice is receiving for the services and materials it provides to its patients such as exam fees, contact lens sales, glasses sales and goodwill. (*Goodwill* refers to the fair market price of the business minus its actual assets, intangible assets and liabilities obtained upon purchase. We will explore goodwill further in the Buying a Practice section of this chapter).

Operating cash flow also includes direct payments and insurance payments. *Asset expenditure* refers to necessary expenses in order to generate exam fee revenue and glasses/contact lens sales. This includes equipment purchases and office/ophthalmic supplies.

Profit

Now that we understand equity and cash flow, it is time to get down to the nitty-gritty that we are all concerned about, *profit*. By definition, profit is the difference of *revenue* and *cost of goods sold (COGS)*.

Profit = Revenue - Cost of Goods Sold (COGS)

Revenue represents the gross amount of money brought in from materials and services. *Cost of Goods Sold* includes the money expended on obtaining the materials necessary to produce revenue - such as frames and lenses.

When profit is determined, it is often useful to obtain a key piece of data called a *profit margin.* The profit margin is a ratio and can be calculated with the following equation:

Profit Margin = Profit / (Revenue x 100)

Profit can be further broken down into two types:

Gross profit strictly shows us the money we bring following the subtraction of cost of goods sold. This is a good starting point, but does not truly show us the money we are actually making.

Net profit fills this void. Net profit can often take a variety of meanings, but for the sake of its application to an optometric business, it represents the revenue left over *after all costs of doing business are negated.* These costs of doing business include cost of good sold, rent/mortgage, utilities, office supplies and staff payroll. (Basically, everything except your personal pay.)

Depreciation and Amortization

We have thrown the words depreciation, amortization and goodwill around in the previous paragraphs, and chances are, you have heard these words in relation to business accounting. So, what do they mean?

Depreciation is defined as a reduction in the value of a *tangible asset* over time, most often due to wear and tear of the asset. A *tangible asset* in an optometrist's case refers to equipment. Depreciation plays an important role in optometric practice, because all our equipment depreciates! Just like a brand-new BMW (which a financially savvy optometrist like yourself should already know not to purchase), your OCT, fundus camera and even your direct ophthalmoscope all lose value the second you purchase them. But depreciation is not all bad news. Claiming depreciation allows for tax breaks by being used as a *write-off*. When this is done correctly, it can benefit your practice greatly.

Amortization is defined as the process of allocating the cost of *intangible assets* over a period of time and may also refer to the repayment of loan principal over time. So, what is the difference between amortization and depreciation? *Basically, the difference between tangible versus intangible assets.*

An *intangible asset* refers to assets that are not physical, and include goodwill, brand recognition and business methodology (in other businesses, trademarks and patents are also included under this), while a tangible asset is physical.

Profit & Loss Statements and Balance Sheets

Now that we have thoroughly enriched our business acumen with an exciting vocabulary and formula list, let us explore how we (or more likely our accountants) can actually apply these terms on paper.

A **profit & loss (P&L) statement** summarizes the revenues, expenses and costs that are incurred over *a period of time*, most commonly a fiscal year or quarter.

Take a look at a sample P&L statement below:

Profit & Loss
January through December 2018

	Jan - Dec 18
Ordinary Income/Expense	
Income	
Fee for Service Income	408,034.98
Fee for Service Income - C-C...	682,428.01
Interest Income	7.70
Total Income	1,090,470.69
Expense	
Advertising and Promotion	569.47
Amortization Expense	27,367.00
Business Licenses and Perm...	493.75
Contact Lenses	157,133.53
Depreciation Expense	22,000.00
Equipment Lease	33,920.10
Finance Charges	0.00
Frames	112,170.47
Freght - Out	140.42
Freight - In	408.66
inssurance Liability AOA	112.00
Insurance - Health	27,448.40
Insurance - Liability	1,159.00
Insurance - Malpractice	720.00
Insurance - Worker Comp	2,021.00
Interest Expense - Stearns B...	1,173.43
Interest Expense - Wells Fargo	28,082.90
Internet	928.50
Laboratory Fees	43,527.71
Maintenance and Repair	202.26
Marketing and Promotion	4,157.32
Meals and Entertainment	45.75
Membership	6,525.51
Merchant Account Fees	14,195.46
Office Expense	4,170.85
Office Supplies	5,144.71
Payroll Expenses	384,114.14
Payroll Taxes	5.82
Postage & Delivery	5,091.14
Professional Fees	34,725.00
Professional License	440.00
Property Tax	1,295.88
Regular lenses	37,361.58
Rent Expense	71,586.00
Security Alarm	351.00
Service Fee - Coding	0.00
Taxes	800.00
Telephone Expense	4,303.09
Utilities	
Trash	405.77
Utilities - Other	4,311.34
Total Utilities	4,717.11
Website	278.75
Total Expense	1,038,887.71
Net Ordinary Income	51,582.98
Net Income	51,582.98

By looking at a P&L statement we can visualize where all our business's cash is going. This statement can show us particular areas where we may be spending too much and gives us good ratios on each aspect of capital expenditure.

A **balance sheet** is a complete record of assets and liabilities. Essentially the assets and liabilities should equal each other achieving balance, hence the naming of this form. Remember our Accountant's Formula at the beginning of this chapter? This is basically that equation in long form.

Now that we have the basics of business under our belt, it is time to analyze.

Now it is time to make a choice. Blue pill or red pill?

Ok, choosing your route into private practice might not be as exciting as Neo's penultimate decision in *The Matrix*. Or is it?

Blue Pill: Opening Cold

Opening a practice cold is a daunting task to say the least. Recent statistics point to nearly 20% of new businesses failing within a year of opening. Starting a practice from scratch, especially in a profession that has been around for nearly one hundred years is by no means easy. However, it can be done. Thousands of your peers have done it.

Start With Location

In order to create a financially feasible cold start, you'll need to be in the right location. Areas of saturation, such as big cities present a multitude of competition. Worse yet, established competition presents an even tougher nut to crack. On the flipside, desolate areas may seem like a goldmine, but it is always important to note if you will have a big enough population to support you.

When searching for an area to lay down your foundation, carefully scan these items:

1) Demographics - Including types of households (ex: young families, singles, elderly), languages spoken other than English and the general culture of the community.

2) Income level - Are you banking on Medicaid exams or Gucci frames? Sure, you offer advanced dry eye therapy, but does anyone have the disposable income to pay for it?

3) Competition - Pay attention to density, location and reputation. You don't want to open up shop next to another OD, but if he sucks at refracting, he could be your new patient source.

Develop Your Niche

While cold starting as a do-it-all type private practice that offers every service under your state's scope may seem like the best way to get patients through your door, this may not always be the case. Examine the population demographic that you are moving into carefully. Catering services that appeal to your demographic and also to yourself will help you build a far more successful practice that you will enjoy running. Are you opening up in a retirement community? A dry eye and glaucoma niche may be up your alley. Are you opening up near a local high school? Consider vision therapy or sports vision.

Now this is not to say that you cannot build a general primary care practice. Ultimately, this will be the core of your patient base and bottom line. However, establishing a niche will help you stand out amongst the myriad of competition and blandness. It will establish your brand and your name.

Find a Lease or Invest in a Building

When finding a location for your practice, it is important to consider the amount of cash you need to put towards occupancy costs. Your lease or mortgage payment will be a set cost to you whether you are making money or losing money.

Choosing whether to lease or own is highly dependent on available real estate and available capital. Ownership presents the opportunity to build equity in real estate, but also comes with a higher initial cost.

Selecting your building is just the beginning. Unless the building is a turnkey optometry office, you will need to dedicate significant amount of capital to a build out for exam lanes, optical, reception and lab.

Start Lean

There are **two ways** you are starting your practice cold:

1) You are using your ***OWN CAPITAL*** either gained through prior work or through borrowing from family or friends

2) You took out a ***LOAN*** (mostly likely a Small Business Loan) to finance the start of your business. Right from the get-go you are slapped with some major negative cash flow. *Is this a bad thing? Not at all!* But it does mean you need to be careful with the limited funds you have. "**Spending lean" is key.**

However, do not skimp or cut corners. Make sure you have the necessary tools needed to adequately treat your patients. Try to hash out discounts where possible and also look to buy local. This will help you establish relationships with other local retailers, which will help build your patient base.

Create a Budget

Without a budget, your debt potential becomes endless. This is not a good situation! Before you beginning purchasing items such as equipment, office supplies, furniture and decorations; write a budget for these items to prevent overspending.

Write Up a Business Plan

A key part in starting a business is priming yourself with goals you wish to achieve and outlining your proposed methods of achieving these. Essentially, this is your business plan. Pick up a book on writing a business plan or Google some sample business plans.

There is no need for the business plan to be excessive or overly detailed! Simply outline your plans and methods for growing your practice and includes some projections. Often when applying for loans (especially with larger banks), a business plan will be a necessary, and often required, part of your pitch.

Finally, Make Sure You are Financially Fit Enough to make the leap

Opening a practice cold is a huge risk. Make sure you have the appropriate means to react to situations that are less than stellar. Continue to build a bank of solid personal wealth while opening cold. This includes paying down student loans, saving for retirement and maintaining an emergency fund. Many times, opening cold requires moonlighting at other established practices just to make ends meet. This might translate to working seven days a week.

Remember that no business becomes successful overnight. Avoid falling into the trap of analyzing the short term; rather focus on the long term. With persistence and consistency, you will tip the scales in your favor.

Red Pill: Purchasing an Existing Practice

The flipside to starting a private practice is to purchase an existing one. Purchasing a practice is a daunting task, however if done correctly, it can produce a huge return on investment. You must evaluate the ins and outs of a potential practice. This includes cash flow, growth potential, bottom lines, net income ratios, prior liabilities assumed and many other aspects.

So how do we go about placing a fair market value on a practice and subsequently purchasing a practice? Well, there are a few steps to take:

(I) Get a Third-Party Appraisal
(II) Do Your Due Diligence
(III) The Four Methods of Valuing a Practice

(IV) Assets vs. Stock Purchase

In the next section, we will explore each of these steps in depth.

(I) Get a Third-Party Appraisal

If you are seriously considering purchasing a practice, always hire a third party appraiser. While there are no stringent guidelines for an appraiser, always look for experience when finding an appraiser. The higher the quantity and variation of valuations that an appraiser has under his/her belt, the better results will be. Hiring a third-party appraiser offers three distinct benefits to the purchase process:

1) It gives an unbiased, "expert" opinion on what the practice is worth

In this chapter, I'll give you a variety of ways to calculate the value of a practice. When you calculate the value of a practice you want to buy, you will inevitably calculate a lower number and the seller will calculate a higher number. This is why you need a third opinion.

2) It gives you a basis for negotiation

When negotiating, a solid number from an unbiased source provides a sort of "pillar" to work around. If that pillar favors you, then even better!

3) It may uncover some devilish details

In order to provide you the best valuation, a good appraiser will sort through a ton of numbers and spreadsheets. Since this is their line of work, they may find less than stellar liabilities or business practices may have slipped in between the cracks when you did your own due diligence.

(If you are looking for OD's on Finance-approved appraisers, visit odsonfinance.com and click on the "Recommended" tab.)

(II) Do Your Due Diligence

Due diligence is defined as reasonable steps taken by a person in order to satisfy a legal requirement, especially in buying or selling something. When purchasing a practice, due diligence encompasses three important steps:

1) Obtaining and analyzing financial documents from the last three years

- Tax Returns
- Profit and Loss statements, cash flow statements
- Frame/Contact Lens Inventory
- Equipment Inventory records
- Lab Inventory records
- Building lease/mortgage
- Legal documents
- Employee demographics and any special circumstances pertaining to employees

2) Analyzing the flow, mechanics and chemistry of the practice

- Take some time to be in the office and learn how it runs, often times, it is best if you have worked as an associate in the office

- Take special notes on ruts and potholes that slow the office down or cause it to lose profitability - will you be able to fix these when you take over?

3) Analyze future profitability and growth potential

- Consider the economics and demographics of an area. Is population and industry steadily growing, like Fremont, CA? Or is it rapidly declining, like Gary, IN? This will play directly into your bottom-line.

- How many patients will leave when the practice switches hands?

- What is each patient worth? - Will you have to see 40 Medicaid patients a day or can you swing 6 multi-pair cash patients a day to make ends meet?

Due diligence is a process. It is not something that should be done overnight. It should be methodical, and should optimally involve help from an accountant, lawyer and appraiser. Read through documents carefully and study every aspect of the practice. If you plan to invest a sizeable amount of capital into an already established business, you want to make sure it will give a good return on investment.

Here is a laundry list of all necessary items to obtain from a potential seller (and his/her accountant) in order to perform due diligence. If possible, involve your accountant, lawyer, appraiser and any potential practice management personnel in the process of due diligence

Due Diligence Laundry List
1) Last 3 years tax statements
2) Last 3 years profit and loss statements
3) Local demographics of area
4) Pictures/video of office, surrounding area and optical (if remote individuals involved)
5) Frame inventory
6) Lens inventory (if edging)
7) Contact lens inventory
8) Equipment inventory and value
9) Lab equipment inventory and value
10) Value of leasehold improvements (depreciated for wear)
11) Office equipment and furniture value
12) Fee schedule
13) Total full exams last 3 years
14) Total new exams last 3 years
15) Employee demographics (positions/age/salary/years with the practice)
16) Any special circumstances with staff (relation to Drs, etc.)
17) Lease arrangement, length, rate

(III) The Four Methods of Valuing a Practice

There are a myriad of ways to calculate the value of the practice. Although some methods may be used more than others, there is no "100% correct way" of valuing a practice. Ultimately, the value of a practice becomes a mutual agreement between the potential seller and potential buyer. The buyer assumes it to be a price that will demonstrate a substantial return, while the seller assumes it will be a price that is fair, considering the potential that has been built. Let's dive into the methodologies used to calculate a practice's value.

There are Four Total Accepted ways to derive the value of a practice. Each method provides a distinct perspective on revenue.

Methods of Valuing a Practice
• **Revenue Stream Method**
• **Capitalization of Earnings Method**
• **Net Plus Assets Method**
• **Debt Service Model Method**

1) Revenue Stream Method

It is common practice to evaluate a practice based on a percentage of the previous year's gross collections. In fact, the Journal of the American Optometric Association states that "The average practice valuation of optometric practices... is *58.7% of gross income* of the year preceding the sale of the practice...(others) have noted that the price paid for a practice is typically *40% to 70% of the gross income* of the year preceding the sale of the practice..."

In order to derive your percentage multiplier of gross income, it is important to go through a careful analysis of expenses in all major categories to make sure they are within normative values for an office of its size, location and demographic. Many things must be considered when benchmarking practice norms and the "zip code" is of great significance.

It is expected that a practice in the rural Midwest will net a significantly higher amount than a practice in a major metropolitan area. The cost of staffing and occupancy can be as much as 10% higher for these urban areas and as a result will have a direct effect on the net income of the practice as well as the valuation itself.

Occupancy expenses including staffing costs are other important factors to look at when using the Revenue Stream Method. Also, cost of goods sold plays a factor. All these aspects of a practice are linked to net income, which in turn casts its large shadow over picking your percentage multiplier of gross.

Revenue Stream Method
Purchase Price = 58.7% or X of Gross Revenue
(X being adjusted based on a variety of cash flow factors)

2) Capitalization of Earnings Method

The Capitalization of Earnings Method is a common method, which attempts to convert the practice income stream into a single lump sum value that represents both goodwill and assets of a practice. In other words, *what would be a reasonable amount for a buyer to pay to receive a projected annual profit?*

To create this scenario, this method compares the practice as an investment as compared to alternative investments available to a potential purchaser. The formula for Capitalization of Earnings Method is listed below:

Capitalization of Earnings Method
Purchase Price = Adjusted Earnings/Capitalization Rate

Now, here are a few definitions that will help you better understand this formula.

Adjusted Earnings = the true earnings of the owner of the practice, minus the cost of paying an optometrist's reasonable compensation to provide services in the owner's practice.

145

Earnings are not merely judged by the amount of the salary paid to the owner. It includes several benefits that have monetary value to them, including but not limited to: personal health insurance, automobile expenses, continuing education, retirement plans and even loan payments that go to increase the level of the owner's equity.

Capitalization Rate - The capitalization rate, or "cap rate", is a numeric value derived to approximate the risk associated with the continuation of the cash flow of the practice. This is usually derived as a percentage that the earnings are divided by to determine the final value of the practice. The most common method of determining the cap rate evaluates the different risk factors of investing in an optometric practice versus other forms of investments such as mutual funds, stocks, etc.

Elements that increase the risk of purchasing a particular practice will decrease its value, and vice versa. However, many of the risk factors associated with the purchase of a professional practice versus the purchase of other types of investments can be considered benign.

For example, a given buyer could find several risk factors such as demographics or heavy competition negligible if they are set on a certain geographic area.

Here are some of the risk factors considered in determining the capitalization rate for a given practice:
- Area demographics
- Physical office location
- Competition from area eye professionals
- Financial production and trends
- Patient flow – both new and existing patients
- Seller / Bank financing
- Number of years in business at present location
- Value of medical and office equipment
- Existing and future lease terms

3) Net Plus Assets Method

Net Plus Assets Method
Purchase Price = Average Adjusted Profit + Physical Asset Value

A time proven method of appraisal that weighs heavily on the actual physical assets of the practice is the net plus assets method. Traditionally, the asset value is determined from information obtained from depreciation schedules on the company tax returns. The condition of the equipment and leasehold improvements can also be taken from those values. It should be noted that unless an individual's evaluation of each asset was performed, it would be impossible to ascertain their exact value.

Here is a list of specific asset values to look at:
1. **Equipment**
2. **Furnishings**
3. **Inventory values**
4. **Leasehold improvements**

At the time of closing, it is recommended that another inventory be performed and if the value is 10% greater or less than the published value below a compensatory adjustment should be made to the final purchase price.

4) Debt Service Model Method

The debt service model looks at the ability of the business to service debt above reasonable compensation for optometric services. The model uses a term of 10 years at 5.0% interest representing standard financing terms in the commercial lending market today for a practice with similar cash flow and asset values that exceed goodwill.

Debt Service Model
Purchase Price = (Annual Adjusted Earnings x 10 years) - 5% Fixed Interest Rate for 10 years

(IV) Assuming Liability When Purchasing a Practice

When purchasing a practice, you will most likely be presented with two options: an asset purchase or a stock purchase. An **asset sale** is the purchase of individual *assets* and liabilities, whereas a **stock sale** is the purchase of the owner's shares of a corporation.

An *asset sale generally favors the buyer* because the seller retains long-term debt obligations and implied tax advantages due to the ability to re-depreciate certain assets. A *stock sale generally favors the seller* because this type of sale typically gets taxed at a *lower capital gains rate* plus the buyer does not get the ability to re-depreciate certain assets.

If the business in question is a sole proprietorship, a partnership, or a limited liability company (LLC), the transaction cannot be structured as a stock sale since none of these entity structures have stock.

Instead, owners of these entity types can sell their partnership or membership interests as opposed to the entity selling its assets. If the business is incorporated, either as a regular C-corporation or as a sub-S corporation, the buyer and seller must decide whether to structure the deal as an asset sale or a stock sale.

Structuring your Business

So, you have officially bought or started your optometric practice. Now it is time to structure your business in a way that is beneficial to you tax wise while protecting you as an individual. The first necessary tool in starting your business is **incorporating.**

A quick disclaimer before reading the rest of this section - laws that govern how you can structure your optometric practice from a business standpoint vary state by state. This section is meant to be a general guide to familiarize you with incorporation and different business entities. Please check your state laws and with a lawyer/CPA before making decisions regarding information discussed in this section.

While incorporating can be done on your own, the better way is to just have a lawyer do it. Sure, it will cost more money, but you will be sure that it is done correctly and in harmony with the law. Once you have your **Articles of Incorporation**, you now need to structure your business entity.

Business entities come in various forms and shapes. In fact, there are 5 entities that are commonly used to structure an optometric business:
- **Sole proprietor**

- **Partnership**

- **Limited Liability Company (LLC)**

- **S-Corp**

- **C-Corp**

While one entity might seem like a logical step for one type of practice, it may not be suited for another practice. Let's go into a brief overview of the various types of business entities.

Sole Proprietor

Sole proprietor is a type of enterprise that is owned and run by one natural person and in which there is no legal distinction between the owner and the business entity. The owner is in direct control of all elements and is legally accountable for the finances of such business and this may include debts, loans, loss, etc.

The sole trader receives all profits (subject to taxation specific to the business) and has unlimited responsibility for all losses and debts. Every asset and debt belongs to the proprietor.

A sole proprietor may use a trade name or business name other than his, her, or its legal name. In some areas, they may have to legally trademark their business name if it differs from their own legal name.

The main benefit of being a sole proprietor is the ease and simplicity of the system. Everything runs through you and thus you can control and understand your business in a manageable way. The glaring negative with sole proprietorship is the **_huge amount of liability_** from your business that you assume as an individual.

Partnership

A partnership is an arrangement where parties, known as partners, agree to cooperate to advance their mutual interests of a business. Partnerships can be further broken down into General Partnerships and Limited Partnerships.

- **General Partnership (GP)** is a partnership in which general partners share equally in both responsibility and liability. It must be created by two or more individuals in agreement, have proof of existence and estoppel.

- **Limited Partnership (LP)** is similar to a GP except that there must be at least one general partner and one limited partner. A limited partner (aka "silent partner) is someone whose liability is limited to his or her investment in the business. Because the limited partner isn't a significant owner, IRS considers their income to be taxed as _passive income._

C-Corporation

A C-Corporation refers to any corporation that is taxed separately from its owners. A C-corporation is distinguished from an S-corporation, which generally is not taxed separately. Most major companies (and many smaller companies) are treated as C-corporations for U.S. federal income tax purposes. C-corporations and S-corporations both enjoy limited liability, but only C-corporations are subject to corporate income taxation.

S-Corporation

S-Corporation is a closely held corporation (or, in some cases, a limited liability company (LLC) or a partnership) that makes a valid election to be taxed under Subchapter S of Chapter 1 of the Internal Revenue Code. In general, S-corporations do not pay any income taxes. Instead, the corporation's income or losses are divided among and passed through to its shareholders. The shareholders must then report the income or loss on their own individual income tax returns.

Limited Liability Company/Professional Limited Liability Company (LLC)

A limited liability company (LLC) is a hybrid legal entity having certain characteristics of both a corporation and a partnership or sole proprietorship (depending on how many owners there are).

An LLC is a type of unincorporated association distinct from a corporation. The primary characteristic an LLC shares with a corporation is limited liability, and the primary characteristic it shares with a partnership is the availability of pass-through income taxation, meaning that income of the business is filed as part of the owner's personal income and not taxed separately.

Did the last few paragraphs make you fall asleep? Well, here's a grid summary with extra details to help you fall into a deeper slumber:

Business Entity	Definition	Pros	Cons
Sole Proprietor	Owned and run by one natural person in which there is no legal distinction between the owner and the business entity	-Complete control over business -Unlimited liability could mean extended credit from creditors -You receive all business profits	-Personally liable for all business debts -Harder to raise capital and get loans -Creditors can go after personal property/assets
Partnership	Partners (more than one individual) share responsibility and liability of the business entity; can be GP or LP	-Shared costs and responsibility -Complementary skills -Each partner controls part of business	-Jointly liable -Partners are personally liable for debts -Profit sharing/lack of control
LLC	Unincorporated hybrid of corporation and partnership/sole proprietorship	-Flow-through income taxation -Less paperwork, low filing costs -Members protected from some liabilities	-As an LLC member you cannot pay yourself wages -Franchise/ capital taxes (varies by state) -Renewal fees/publication requirements (varies by state)
C-Corp	Limited liability corporation taxed separately from owners	-Personal asset protection -Pass through taxation -Credibility to public -Easy to transfer ownership	-Formation is tricky -Stock restrictions due to pass through -Less flexible -Tax obligations - IRS monitors more closely
S-Corp	Closely held corporation or LLC, income tax divided/passed through shareholders	-No double taxation -Protects liability -Room for investors -Easier accounting rules	-Rules and fees -Shareholder restrictions -Salary requirements for officers

Keeping Your Practice Profitable

How do I make and keep a business profitable? Well, that's the million-dollar question. Literally.

Business profitably is the subject of many books, magazines, Internet blogs and newspaper articles. (Heck, when this book is published, I will have written 20 articles for various optometric business publications regarding profitability).

You can pay enormous amounts of money to attend seminars on how to be more profitable. You can find numerous Podcasts and YouTube stations dedicated solely to this subject. In fact, one could write a whole book, or possibly a series of books on the topic.

However, since this is merely a chapter in a book with a much broader scope, I am going to attempt to breakdown efficient practice profitability into *5 Tenets*. These 5 Tenets have worked to make my own private practice profitable. I learned and employed these Tenets through mentors (whom consequently also ran massively successful practices), a plethora of business and marketing books (in fact, each of these Tenets has *whole books* dedicated to them) and through trial and quite a bit of error on my part.

The 5 Tenets of Practice Profitability
- Create Systems for *Consistency and Efficiency*
- Find Your *Most Profitable Revenue Streams* and Exploit Them
- *Reduce Costs*
- *Brand Yourself*
- Be Different - *Aim for Vertical*, not Lateral Growth

1) Create Systems for Consistency and Efficiency

Are you practice owner and do not have a practice handbook? Fix that now. Your first step towards creating a synergistic and productive practice revolves around having a common law, in print that allows everyone to operate on the same page. For the same reason, the Bible was written for the world and the Constitution for the US, a practice handbook allows your small biosphere of doctors, opticians, billers and receptionist to have *set methodology to streamline operations.*

The primary thesis of Michael Gerber's popular *E-Myth* series, having a manual for operations allows you to deliver consistent service and goods which are important to keeping your efficiency and to your patient's satisfaction. The key is **consistency.** The reason that mega corporations like McDonalds and Apple operate so successfully is the *consistency of their products and services.*

Practice Profitability Pro-Tip #1: *Develop a specific and efficient system that values consistency*

However, in order to deliver this consistency (and consequent efficiency), you must study what works and what does not work. Then, you need to break it down. And continue to break it down. You want baby steps otherwise this Tenet falls apart. Take for instance, a task as simple as answering a phone. Multiple studies have shown that every successful business will have the same phone greeting. Not just the words, *but also the intonation of the answerer and the timing. If* any of these are thrown off, this can actually affect a caller in a negative way.

2) Find Your Most Profitable Revenue Streams and Exploit Them

In order to get your practice to be truly financially efficient, you need to break apart your various profit streams. Break it down into services, glasses, contacts and miscellaneous items. Then break it down further - we're talking small details. Analyze your services in detail. What are you pulling in net profits for such items like exams, ancillary tests, specialty contact lens fittings, glaucoma work ups or vision therapy? Analyze your optical. Are you selling high end or low end? Progressives with antireflective coatings or single vision CR-39?

Now, it is time to go one step deeper. *Analyze your demographics.* I do not mean going on Google and finding out how many college grads are in your area (although this may be useful information). I mean go into your EMR (or your paper books if you're old school) and find **who your top earners are.** Start with the top 100 of your highest grossing patients. Find out what services they got and what they bought. Next, *find out what makes them happy.* This is key. (Side note: most EMR software packages have tools to do this)

You may have heard of the **Pareto Principle**, also known as the 80/20 Rule, the law of the vital few, or principle of factor scarcity.

First of all, if a rule has four different names - it must have some validity. *Basically, the Pareto Principle states that 80% of your production (money) comes from 20% of your assets (patients) and vice versa.* The Pareto Principle has been proven to be a known phenomenon in a wide range of businesses and also in various facets of science such as horticulture.

Practice Profitability Pro Tip #2: *Find your top 100 patients, study every trend and demographic about them and use this information to market and gain patients of similar value*

The Pareto Principle not only applies to patients that give more in the money aspect, it also applies to patients that give more in the time aspect. In this sense, we're looking at the 20% in a negative light, since they will be taking 80% of your time. If you are encountering patients like this that are hindering your productivity and subsequently making you hate your job, make notes! Consider forgetting to send that recall card or phone call, and instead fill up that time thief's time slot with one of your newly gained patients from Pro Tip #2.

Want to read about the Pareto Principle and exploiting profitable revenue streams ad naseum? Pick up *The 4 Hour Work Week* by Tim Ferriss to learn more about applying the principle to time management and your career.

3) Reduce Costs

If you are reading this chapter while sitting in your leather Herman Miller executive chair with your feet propped on your ivory-embellished mahogany desk inside your large Doctor's office inside your practice, I have one question for you.

What the hell are you thinking?

Your practice is a space for generating as much quality patient care and income as possible. That means you need to eliminate all the extra crap and unnecessary luxuries. If anything, these unnecessary items pose a detriment not only to your cash flow, but also to your useable space.

One of the saddest conversations I have with fellow practice owners is that they are hardly taking a decent paycheck home from their practice that appears to be thriving on the surface. Some of these practitioners have established practices that have been running for years! In the few instances I have gotten to analyze the books, the problem is almost always the same: cash flow is low and often thwarted by a barrage of expenses.

On many occasions, I have brought this up with a practice owner and I am met with the same old excuse *"But our cash is good, our collections are awesome, I see so many patients. What are you talking about?"*

Well the problem is, cash doesn't tell the story.

Cash is garbage. *Cash Flow is king*

Wow, Aaron put that in a "memorize this!" box so it must be important...but it looks like some mantra someone superimposed onto a picture of mansion and Lamborghini and posted on Instagram.

Well yes, I actually did first come across the saying in the aforementioned Instagram post (thanks Grant Cardone), however the words ring true. *Cash is nothing if it is constantly burned and leaked out. Cash doesn't make you rich because it is transient. Cash flow is truly king.*

So, how do we lean out your practice to make it a lean, efficient, positive cash flow machine? The first step is to set up a budgeting system in which you **pay yourself first**.
"Wait, I'm the owner, I'm the first one to take the fall when the going gets tough."

No. And here's why. When you pay yourself first, you create a system where you must both understand and actively manage your purchases/expenses. When you are left with a smaller amount of cash, rather than a larger amount of cash you are more likely to make frugal, and frankly better choices to make your dollar go further. This is called the **scarcity principle**, which is a real term used in social psychology and business disciplines.

Think about it this with toothpaste. When you have a full tube of toothpaste you use it liberally, often putting more than you need on your toothbrush, sharing with others and not minding if some drops into the sink. However, what happens when that tube is near empty? You all of sudden become the most frugal dental hygiene expert ever, finding multiple ways to squeeze that last little morsel out.

So how do you do it? Some methods advocate for separate bank accounts in which you place set amounts for expenses, rent, etc. The key to making this work is to decide on a set amount to pay yourself (make it reasonable) as well as set amounts to divvy up for different expenses. Remember that this method will require you to be creative in order to spend less to make more. If you want a whole book on how paying yourself and using the scarcity principle can dramatically increase cash flow, check out *Profit First* by Mike Michalowicz.

4) Brand Yourself

Just do it. The ultimate driving machine. The social network. What do all these short phrases have in common? Well, you know exactly what company they refer to. But it goes deeper than sloganeering something memorable. We know brands because we instantly associate them with a proposed category of **value**. The key factor for branding to work is for the consumer or patient to understand that the underlying experience behind the nifty niche fitting will be beneficial.

When it comes to optometry, branding types can be seen in practice and parallels can be drawn to major publicly traded companies. Many business and marketing gurus break branding into three categories for optometry practices:

The Three Types of Optometric Branding
Innovation Branding - seen in companies such as Apple, *technology and exclusivity* create demand and allow *high cost* of sales of a *few items*
Value Branding - seen in companies such as Walmart, *good deals and supposed savings* create demand and allow *low cost* of sales on a *high volume of items*
Luxury/Boutique Branding - seen in companies such as the Ritz-Carlton, *excessive attention to detail and personal needs* create demand and allow for *ultra-high cost* of sales for *very select items*

So, how do these types of branding apply specifically to optometry?

A great example of **Innovation Branding** has been Lenscrafter's ongoing campaign to market the variety of "high tech" machines they use in refraction and in fitting glasses, as well as their in-house lab optical.

Value Branding is commonly used by chain opticals such as Stanton optical and also used by practices in low income, densely populated areas.

Luxury/Boutique branding can be seen in trendy/niche opticals in Beverly Hills or Manhattan.

When devising how your practice will brand itself, consider the three types of branding and even hybridize two of them.[3] Additionally, branding is not limited to these three types; there are many offsets of branding that are constantly being developed as our economy evolves.

Convenience branding is a new type of branding that is being favored by millennials and revolves around Internet commerce and subscription services such as Sightbox or Warby-Parker. This new branding has begun to make its way into optometry.

> **Practice Profitability Pro-Tip #4:** *Brand yourself with one or two branding styles. Do not use more than two styles. Remember that providing value is the core component that will allow your branding to work.*

Once you have decided on the types of branding your practice will follow, it's time to *visually associate this branding.* This includes everything: your logo, your office design and the apparel of your staff to name a few. Choose styling that matches your brand type. If you are an Innovation practice, then futuristic and metallic designs may be more up your alley; if you are a Value practice, then a more simplistic design with green coloration may work better.

5) Be Different - Aim for Vertical, not Lateral Growth

One thing that I've seen far too often with practice owners is the overconfident complacency with status quo. They get into a comfortable routine and just keep going, expecting the giving tree (a.k.a. the practice) to continue producing fruit without applying the proper gardeners touch of watering, sunlight, fertilizing and occasional grafting. There seems to be a static approach to running a practice rather than a dynamic approach.

---

[3] My private practice in Los Altos utilizes a hybrid-branding scheme that heavily favors Luxury/Boutique Branding and also employs Innovation Branding. We do not use Value Branding. This has worked very well for our location in an affluent party of the Bay Area, CA.

*The problem with this approach is that a practice is a **dynamic model.***

Despite the establishment or maturity of a practice, there are too many variables to simply "set the machine and let it run."

Practice Profitability Pro-Tip #5: *The only thing limiting your practice growth is a narrow mindset and static approach. Constantly search for alternatives and don't be afraid to Fail*

I truly believe that any and every practice has the ability to produce **radical growth**, even with the barrage of rising barriers that the industry is now facing that I mentioned in Chapter 1. In order to achieve growth, you need to both outsmart the competition and simply be better than the competition. Adopt a growth mindset with your practice.

Can I increase contact lens sales by offering a deal on plano sunglasses? How about if I start my own webstore and offer contact lenses at a lower price? Other companies do subscription services, why can't I?

There are so many ways you can grow your practice, some of which may have not yet been discovered. Some of your ideas fail, but others will succeed.

The key is to continually try and learn from past failures.

The Optometrist's Guide to Financial Freedom

CHAPTER ELEVEN: Real Estate: "Buying, Renting & Investing" BY: Aaron

"The best investment on earth, is earth."

-Louis Glickman

On your journey to the American Dream, one key hurdle stands in your way - home ownership. Owning a home allows for autonomy in daily living and helps you build equity. It enables you to proudly display the fruits of your hardworking career; four walls, a roof and a floor; that all belong to you. *Unfortunately owning a home also can create insurmountable headaches and envelope you in debt.*

Maybe you already own your home. What about additional properties? If leveraged correctly, investing in real estate can yield you a substantial amount of supplementary income and could eventually become primary income. After reading this chapter, you should be able to answer the following questions:

- **Should I buy a house?**

- **How should I finance my house purchase?**

- **What type of house should I buy?**

- **How does Real Estate investing work?**

- **Is Real Estate investing a good path for me to take?**

Should I buy a House?

The first thing to consider when exploring home ownership is whether you are truly in a financially sound position to own a home and how much home you can actually afford.

When considering the purchase of a home, a thorough analysis of personal finances should be made. Take into account all debt including credit cards, student loans and business debt. Owning a house early presents some great positives - **equity is built early,** money is no longer "thrown away" on rent and tricky moves of less-than-stellar landlord such as rent increases can be avoided.

Ultimately, the best way to purchase a home is in full with cash in order to avoid financing and further debt. However, for many individuals, this simply is not feasible. Rising home prices present too high of a burden that cannot be met with the simple liquidity in a savings account.

Enter the home mortgage.

How Should I Finance my House Purchase?

Banks and financial institutions understand the innate human need for property ownership. Thus, a whole method of financing a house was created. In fact, a whole industry revolves around getting individuals and families approved for loans to buy their dream homes and get out of renting.

Before applying for a mortgage, an important question to ask yourself is:

"How much house can I afford?"

First, analyze how much a down payment will affect your financial wellbeing. If you are pooling money from your retirement savings or emergency fund, it may be wise to wait just a little longer. Next, you want to look at how much your mortgage payment will impact your month to month finances, and if this impact will affect your quality of life (cataract surgery won't fix this version of quality of life).

Remember that your total monthly payment will also include *property tax, homeowner's insurance and HOA dues (if applicable)*, so your monthly mortgage rate is NOT a true representation of your monthly payment.

Now, how do we put what we just described in real world terms? While there may not be an all-inclusive rule for every individual entering a mortgage, the Rule of 28 is a good start to determine if you can afford a house.

> ## The Rule of 28 = *Your monthly mortgage payment should not exceed 28% of your gross monthly income*

Ok, now let's apply the Rule of 28 to a real-life scenario. Say you found your dream home at right around $1,000,000. With 20% down ($200,000), that leaves you with a monthly payment (mortgage +property tax + homeowner's insurance) of roughly *$5500 per month.* Applying the Rule of 28, you would need to make around $20,000 per month ($19,642 exactly) to meet the rule. Shocking right?

Should this rule be set in stone? Not necessarily, you can swing an amount that is slightly above. But be wary of going too high above the 28% factor. Why?

Enter homeowner costs.

Homeowner costs are a very real aspect of owning a home. Painting rooms, landscaping, repairing broken dishwashers, unclogging sinks and redoing roofs are a small myriad of challenges that will present to you as you go through the wonderful process of owning (and not renting) a home. In fact, many experts estimate that *1 to 3% of the purchase price of your home will go into home maintenance costs each year*! Thus, the recommendation is that you should have at least this amount in an emergency savings account in case to prepare for this expense.

Beware of Predatory Mortgage Lenders

"Predatory loans only exist for lower income individuals in ominous and overtly green colored strip mall storefronts with some iteration of "cash" in their name". True or false?

FALSE

Predatory loans exist for high-income professionals too and they most definitely market to your sophisticated nose. Much like Lincoln automobiles cater to a different demographic than Ford automobiles, while essentially being the same product; so, do certain mortgage loans and terms.

Often presented with iterations such as **"Physician's Loan,"** banks will often lure young doctors into predatory loans. They'll tell you can put as little as 3% down and buy your house. They reason that since you are a young, strapping physician; you are a low risk for defaulting since you will be making the big bucks. This marketing, in turn, makes you feel pretty good. *Heck, I can buy a house and this fine lending institution trusts me...because I am a baller doctor.*

Before you fall into the bear trap built with your entitlement and insecurity, look at the numbers! If you really only have to pay 3% (or some other ridiculously small amount) for a down payment, that means it's going to be factored into your monthly mortgage payment! These lenders are experts at forcing the math in their favor. Your interest rate? Undoubtedly, it is going to be *higher than normal,* because contrary to what the bank has made you believe, **you as a doctor are a HIGH risk, not a low risk.**

Then, you need to look at terms. Often, these mortgages contain unfavorable terms such as the dreaded ARM (adjustable rate mortgage). An ARM allows the bank to change the interest rate on your mortgage to *whatever they want.* Be very wary of these.

One last thing that will probably be tacked on to your "doctor loan" is **Private Mortgage Insurance (PMI),** which is a type of insurance that protects the lender from potential default from the borrower. It is basically when the lender doesn't believe in your ability to pay, so they take additional insurance to protect themselves.

PMI is normally calculated as a monthly fee added to your mortgage payment and is often considered when an individual cannot come up with a 20% down payment (though not always the case).

Why PMI? When you do not have 20% of your future home's purchase price up front, you are viewed as a *more risky borrower.* Hell, that Lincoln Navigator is starting to look a lot like a beat up Ford Expedition.

We realize that there are many, many variants of so-called doctor/physician loans out there for home purchase. Many are just as described, while others may offer better terms such as no PMI, but they *often make it up for this by a higher mortgage rate* compared to a standard mortgage given to a qualified buyer. Remember, these guys are experts at tilting the favor toward them.

The most important thing is to read the fine print and details if you consider going this mortgage route. Know what you are getting into. Also, know what the future holds. Some plans may switch from a fixed to ARM after a certain amount of years (a 5/1 model is common for this). Will you be able to handle a sudden upswing in interest rate without going through foreclosure, five or ten years down the line? These are things to consider before affixing your John Hancock to that alluring piece of paper.

Your Home is Not an Investment

If you read any real estate investment book, you will undoubtedly see the phrase "your home is not an investment." This may lead you through anger, denial and possibly resentment. *I'm building equity! Why is my home not investment?* Well, here are 5 reasons:

1) It has substantial Carrying Costs
2) It does NOT generate Cash Flow
3) Taking loans against your home will only hurt you
4) Appreciation is not guaranteed
5) It's not an investment if you never sell it

Ok, real life scenario time. Let's go back to that $1,000,000 house. You are a successful practice owner pulling in a cool $250,000 annually (by the way, this is a completely attainable number for anyone reading this book - *believe in yourself, your craft and your ability to thrive!)*, so you meet the Rule of 28 requirements. Ten years down the line you look up your home value. A whopping $1,300,00! You made $300,000 by just living! Wait, not so fast.

1) It has substantial Carrying Costs
Carrying costs represent the following ancillary costs in addition to the principal of your monthly mortgage payment:
- Interest
- Property tax

- Homeowner's insurance
- Private Mortgage Insurance (PMI)* → *you DO NOT want this!*
- Utilities
- Repairs
- Remodels

2) It does NOT generate Cash Flow

You are living in your house. Unlike a stock or bond, you are not generating cash flow (dividends, interest rates, etc.) with the purchase of your home. A rental property on the other hand, does generate cash flow through rent.

3) Taking Loans against your Home will only Hurt You

The dangerous thinking of your home as an investment often leads individuals to taking loans against their home after it has built equity. These loans can come in the form of a lump sum or a Home Equity Line of Credit (HELOC). While this might help you get out of a pinch, it does create new debt and carries fees.

4) Appreciation is not Guaranteed

A common misconception made when buying a house is that there will be a steady stream of appreciation throughout the duration of ownership. This simply is not the case. There are many scenarios can occur where a home can *actually depreciate*, have a stagnant value or not appreciate quicker than the rate of inflation.

5) It is not an investment if you never sell it

Many individuals who buy homes will live in that same home for the rest of their life. If you never sell your home or rent your home, then it never generates any sort of income for you.

What Type of House Should I Buy?

A common question that presents itself to first time homebuyers is: "go big or go small?" *Going big* means buying your long-term home. One that is big enough to accommodate your current needs and your future needs (wife, kids, extended family, etc.). Buying big does come with a price, which is usually a higher monthly mortgage rate and down payment required.

Going small means buying what is called a "starter home." A starter home normally represents a cheaper option than the big home. Sometimes this means a condo or townhouse. Other times this may mean a small single-family home or a fixer upper.

First Home	Pros	Cons
Go Big	-Set for life (or a long time) -Possibility to build higher equity -Don't have to deal with a second home in the future -No moving	-Larger mortgage rate and down payment -Extra cash goes into home rather than other investments -No potential rental income in future
Go Small	-Possibility to start building equity earlier (if cannot afford big home) -Eventual rental income or income from appreciation upon sale -Smaller initial mortgage rate/down payment vs. buying bigger	-May prevent possibility of getting mortgage for next home (depending on circumstances) -May never get to the big home based on life circumstances and future finances

How Does *Real Estate Investing* Work and is it a good Path for me?

So now that we have that out of the way, how do we invest in real estate? Plain and simple. Buy property and rent it out. Essentially, the lifeblood of your earnings on real estate investment is two fold: the equity you build with your property (the assumed increase in value of your property) and the cash flow that you collect through rent.

As a doctor, practice owner and investor, I believe that real estate can be a reliable anchor and substantial wealth generator in a well-diversified portfolio. But there is a catch.

Unlike all the other retirement and investment vehicles we have mentioned in previous chapters, real estate is an **ACTIVE investment.** While you can place $50,000 in a low-cost index fund and forget about it, you cannot buy a property for $50,000 and forget about it. Renter relationships, property management, repairs/maintenance and filling vacant properties are just a few important steps that you must be actively engaged in, in order to be a successful real estate investor.

Here are five keys to keep in mind before committing to real estate investing as a portion of your portfolio:

1) You Must Be Actively Engaged in this Investment
2) You Will Deal with REAL People that will give you REAL problems and REAL headaches. (Ask yourself if you want to be a landlord)
3) There are Legal Implications and Substantial Risks
4) Finding a Good Deal on Your Purchase is Pertinent to Success
5) Cash flow is King

Having tenants on your property (properties) will generate income; however, keep in mind that you are dealing with real people. In this age of DIY, drafting leases and other documentation that deals with tenants and your property is definitely something you want to leave to the experts. Always hire the appropriate legal team to help you, so you can avoid unnecessary liability.

If you are entertaining real estate investing as another stream of income, also consider what type of real estate you are investing in. Different areas and different demographics can translate to large differences in realized cash flow. Single-family residences (often abbreviated as SFR), apartment buildings, duplexes, town homes or commercial buildings can all be extremely lucrative or cash-eating abysses based on their surrounding markets.

When finding your first real estate investment, remember the three L's of real estate: *location, location, and location.* Consider the following scenario of buying a single-family home as an investment. Home A is in upper middle-class suburbia, sells for $500,000 and rents for $2500. Home B is in a high crime urban environment, sells for $250,000 and rents for $2500.

Which home is a better investment?

Based on basic mathematics, Home B is much better. But consider the consequences of your *location.* **Home A** is rented by a young professional family. Two kids, a dog and a consistent rent check that is always in your mailbox on the first of the month. The cost of maintaining the home is relatively low maintenance cost of the home save for Little Bella's tendency to write on the walls with brown Sharpie (or was that Rex having digestive issues? Probably better not to know).

Ok now let's look at Home B. Two colleges buddies rent it. Rent checks are consistently late. *The house is a mess.* You've gotten noise complaints for loud parties and what sounded like firecrackers on multiple occasions (yes, you get to deal with that since you are the owner). One day, you decide to check on the house. You nearly faint. There are at least ten people living in the house. And amongst the sea of empty beer bottles and used syringes you look at the kitchen. Is that a meth lab?

All of a sudden, House A looks a lot better, even though it's netting you much less income. And that's the beauty (or ugliness) of an active investment such as real estate. You need to be involved, and often more lucrative cash flow means more physical involvement, which translates to more time. And as we all know, time is money.

How to Determine a Good Real Estate Investment

By now you have come to realize that real estate is not nearly as black and white as other investment vehicles. Discernment, research and gut instinct are all-important factors in determining where to invest. A few rules of thumb are often used by real estate investors in order to gauge whether a property is a good deal that can generate positive cash flow.

Cash Flow is King

If you just read the previous chapter, then you're probably thinking, "Man, this guy is a broken record!" However, cash flow really is a key component to real estate investing. The ultimate goal is to create steady, positive cash flow with a real estate investment.

If you are not buying your real estate investment with cash and are instead mortgaging, then you must do a cash flow analysis. Make sure your net cash flow is positive.

What is the 1% Rule?

The **One Percent Rule** is a good place to start when evaluating potential real estate. Essentially, the 1% Rule ensures that the rent you collect will equal or exceed your mortgage payment. It states to take 1% of the selling price of your newly acquired property and setting that amount as the base level of your rent.

Base Level of Monthly Rent = 1% x Selling Value of Property

Thus, if you bought a home for $400,000, your monthly rent for the property should be around $4000. Obviously, many factors will influence the price you set for rent, including overall demand and competition from other properties, so take the 1% Rule as a screener.

If we go a step further, we can explore the 2% Rule. Much like its little brother, the 2% Rule simply takes 2% of the selling value of property as the minimum rent price. This is defined as a **good** deal by most real estate investment gurus. However, if you are able to swing the 2% Rule, be wary. There are many factors that may eat into your cash flow (remember our story about the Whites and the Pinkmans...don't understand that joke? Watch the show *Breaking Bad*): poor renters, inability to retain renters, property tax, condition of property, damages to property, etc. Be wise and do your due diligence!

What is the Capitalization Rate (CAP)?

Another important term in real estate investing is Capitalization Rate or CAP Rate. The CAP rate takes the ratio of the net operating income of the real estate asset and the original cost or price paid for the piece of real estate.

CAP Rate = <u>Net Operating Income</u>
Original Cost of Real Estate

Keep in mind that we are looking at *Net Operating Income*, not Gross Operating Income.

So, what is a good Cap rate? Well, that very much depends on *location* and the *type of real estate* you possess. There are many great resources online, such as CBRE.com, which can tell you CAP rate statistics for your area and the different types of real estate.

What's one cool thing about knowing the CAP rate of your real estate investment? Well, it can tell you your payback period - the time it will take to capture your original investment price on a piece of property. Consider a $1,000,000 building purchase. At a Cap rate of 10% annually, it should take you about 10 years to regain that $1,000,000 you initially put down to purchase the building.

How do I make Money on Real Estate Investing?

Real estate investing may be a headache; however, it can provide you with a substantial stream of income. In fact, real estate investing allows income through three distinct outlets.

Three Outlets of Real Estate Income:
1) Rent collection
2) Equity (through forced/natural appreciation)
3) Taxes (through depreciation)

Rent collection will obviously be the biggest and most consistent method of income stream through real estate investment. Building equity can occur through forced appreciation and natural appreciation. *Forced appreciation* refers to updates and remodels made to a property that increase its value. *Natural appreciation* refers to the rise in value of a property over time.

Depreciation presents a great way to save on taxes on subsequently put money into your pocket. Just like you can claim depreciation on your aging OCT, you can also claim depreciation on that house you bought. Put these three outlets of income together and multiply them by a small collection of properties. Now, you can see why some of the wealthiest individuals in the world are involved in real estate.

Residential or Commercial...or REITs?

Now that you have a very basic primer on real estate investing, it's time to look at different types of real estate investments you can make.

Residential real estate refers to properties such as single-family residences (SFR), townhouses, duplexes, condos and multi-family residences (MFR) such as apartment buildings. Residential real estate is *valued based on surrounding property values.* Tenants pay rent and utilities may or may not be included. Owners are normally responsible for maintenance and capital expenditures on the property.

Commercial real estate refers to properties such as office buildings, clinics and warehouses and house places of business. Commercial real estate differs from residential real estate in that *it is often valued based on the net operating income and CAP rate, or through the use of a gross rent multiplier.* Thus, the value for commercial real estate revolves around profitability of businesses that occupy the real estate.

Real Estate Investment Trusts (REITs) refer to companies that own and operate income producing real estate. These companies are often public and allow individuals to buy stock in them, creating a "passive method" of investing in real estate. REITs can be a great way to diversify a portfolio. Mutual funds that focus on multiple REITs are also available. Keep in mind that REITs get taxed differently than stocks and are best kept in a Roth account.

Owning the Building that Houses Your Practice

If you are a practice owner, you've inevitably come across the question of owning your own building. Owning your building allows you to avoid the heartburn associated with changing rent prices and gives you a great way to build equity. Essentially, you can become your own landlord. For tax purposes, you can have your practice entity pay you rent for your building that it is housed in. The best way to do this is to create a separate LLC that owns your building. You then pay rent to this LLC from your practice.

A chance to own your building even works in your favor if you choose to sell your practice or practice elsewhere. As long as rent collection is meeting the 1% or 2% rule, your building can turn into a solid investment.

In conclusion, real estate can be a great addition to an ever-growing portfolio. There are three keys to remember when considering real estate:

1) Real Estate investing is active investing and requires much more work than placing funds in investments such as mutual funds
2) Real Estate investing requires research and due diligence. Carefully analyze properties and weigh their pros and cons before pulling the trigger.
3) Owning your own house is not an investment. Additionally, owning a house does not mean financial security if you are saddled with a high mortgage payment.

Check your finances before considering the purchase of a home to make sure you are in a position where home ownership does not cause financial hardship.

The Optometrist's Guide to Financial
Freedom

CHAPTER 12: Insurance: "What happen if I break my Arm?" BY: Dat

"If a child, a spouse, a life partner or a parent depends on you and your income, you need life insurance" – Suze Orman

Have you ever wondered to yourself what would happen if you broke both your hands and could not do refraction for 6 months? Or even worse, got diagnosed with a life-threatening disease that permanently disabled you? Or get sued by that one patient with the missed retinal detachment simply because you were off your A-Game that one day due to a flu?

Life-threatening incidents are rare but can be extremely devastating both to our personal lives and finances. I love the old saying:

"Insurance is like a life jacket. It's a bit of nuisance when you don't need it, but when you do need it, you are more than thankful to have it."

It is like the **Law of Murphy**, which states, *"Anything that can go wrong will go wrong"*. Doctors who are ill prepared are simply one car wreck, one cancer diagnosis, or one house fire away from going bankrupt.

In general, you should **ONLY** *self-insure against the financial-devastating catastrophes such as death, permanent injuries, or expensive personal lawsuits*. Any situations that can result in expensive medical bills, permanent disability, optometry-related lawsuit, destruction of property and other personal liability should be covered.

Your washing machine being broken sucks but it won't financially bankrupt you, so why would anyone pay for consumer warranty insurance?

Insurance is complicated as heck! And can be a touchy topic especially when it comes to whole life insurance. The whole goal of this chapter is to cover essential fundamentals and go over **Seven Types of Insurance** that an optometrist cannot afford to be with, which are:

1. **Malpractice Insurance**

2. **Health Insurance**

3. **Disability Insurance (Long-Term/Short Term)**

4. **Life Insurance**

5. **Car Insurance**

6. **Home Owner's/Renter's Insurance**

7. **Umbrella Insurance**

(1) Malpractice Insurance

Fortunately, by law, malpractice insurance is required to practice optometry. It gives OD the confidence to clinically practice to the highest standard of care without the fear of losing one's license from lawsuits. This will probably be one of the first responsibilities for a new OD graduate; obtaining his or her professional liability insurance.

The great news is that, optometry malpractice is fairly inexpensive compared to other medical professionals (ranging from $300-$800 per year depending on which state and insurer), with heavy discounts usually available for new graduates. Limits are usually available in two amounts coverage: **$1million/$2million or $2million/$4million**. The 1st amount is the maximum amount that the insurance carrier will *pay per claim* and the 2nd amount is the maximum amount the carrier will *pay for all claims* during the policy year. Most doctors will get their malpractice insurance with the American Optometric Association (AOA) Excel program, which usually provides the most affordable, but feel free to shop around.

We always recommend doing the *full maximum coverage of $2/4 Million Limits*. In addition, most optometry employers will cover it for their associates, but if you are doing casual fill-in as a 1099 independent contractor, you will still need to get your own separate policy.

(2) Health Insurance

As a healthcare provider, I am sure you are quite aware of the high cost of medical expenses with your own patients. According to a study by Kaiser, *medical debt contributes to nearly 50% of all bankruptcies in America*. One unexpected medical emergency can lead to hundreds of thousands in medical bills, causing many families to go into debt.

While it is ideal for your employer to pay for your health benefits, it is more common nowadays for many young doctors to work for a private optometry office that does not offer any health benefits. Many young graduates will start out as a 1099 independent contractor working at two or *even three part time positions* at multiple location.

Even with the rising high cost of medical insurance, it is still unacceptable for any individual to NOT have medical coverage. If you are in relatively good health and don't go to the doctor that often, but just want to insure yourself against extreme life-threatening medical costs, then a *high deductible or catastrophe-only plan is ideal for you.*

With a high-deductible plan, you are responsible for more of your up-front health cost (like higher office visit co-pay) but you will pay a *lower monthly premium* (cost of the insurance each month). Usually a high-deductible plan expects you to pay for all your medical expenses up to a certain amount per year (Example: $2,000 deductible limit). Then anything above the $2,000 limit, the health insurance will cover the rest. Remember:

The higher your yearly deductible limit is, the lower your monthly premium will be.

Also, one great advantage of having a high-deductible health plan is that it allows you to open a Health-saving account (HSA) that is tax-advantaged saving account. HSA can be used specifically for paying medical expenses. As you probably remember in our Retirement chapter, HSA can also acts as a "Stealth IRA" which is another source for retirement.

If you are older or simply have a lot of chronic illness requiring more medical expenses (thus exceeding the high deductible limit) then it is recommended that you sign up for a *higher* monthly premium plan. You will pay more each month for the higher cost insurance plan, but will save money in the long term.

(3) Long-Term Disability Insurance

This is definitely the *most underrated* but most important type of insurance for a practicing optometrist. But unfortunately, it is also the most complicated policy. Long-term disability insurance protects you for a loss of income if you are unable to work for a long period of time (greater than 90 days) due to any illness or injury.

Studies have showed that around **20% of people will have a period of disability before reaching age 65**. So, with those odds, it is simply dumb not to insure against this impeding financial catastrophe.

Disability insurance is extremely convoluted and subjective to each person's health situation, and will vary greatly with each insurer. This chapter is in *no way* a comprehensive summary of all the little nuances that go into each disability policy but will strictly serves as a basic guideline, especially for new doctors.

Disability insurance is sold in direct relations to a certain % of your income and *will get more expensive as you get older, due to a higher chance of insurance payout.* There are many factors that can increase how much you will have to pay such as having a higher risk profession like stuntman, perilous hobbies like rock climbing or sky diving and overall general health. There are furthermore a bunch of exclusion factors as well such as life-threatening medical health rejections that the insurance won't cover within your policy.

For example, if you have a chronic heart condition at the time of the issuing of the disability insurance, but then later on develop a disability due to said a heart attack; the policy is **NOT going to pay you anything** (Crazy right?). Also, there might be other limitations on payout qualifications such as getting injured during foreign travel, pregnancy or mental disorder. The list can go on and on...

How Much Long-Term Disability (LTD) Insurance should you Purchase?

Unlike life insurance, there is *a strict limit* to how much disability insurance you can purchase. As a general rule, most insurance companies will only cover a maximum limit of ***66% of your total salary*** but with an annual ***cost of 1-3% of your total annual salary.***

We usually recommend:

Long Term Disability Insurance Coverage= 60% of pretax Salary

Example: A doctor making $150,000 salary might have an average yearly payment of $3,000 (1-3% of salary) with an average monthly payment of $250. If he is fully disabled and unable to work, his insurance will pay him roughly $90,000 a year (or 60% of his salary), until he is 65-year-old.

There are **5 main factors** that can affect your rate of the policy and can significantly increase the cost.

1) Coverage Amount: How much you need per month when you are not collecting your normal paycheck. *The more you need, the higher cost your insurance rate will be.*

2) Benefit Period: How long you want the benefits to last. This can range from a few years to 10 years, or even until retirement. The longer you want to able receive benefits, the more it will cost. *We recommend a minimum of at least 5 years, but if you can afford more! Go for it!*

3) Waiting Period: The time period between when you become disabled and when you want to start receiving disability benefits. *The shorter the waiting period, the more the policy will cost.* To offset this waiting period, a lot of doctors will usually have enough emergency funds (3-6 months) to cover their expenses, or sign up for short-term disability insurance (discussed later). *We just recommend having a larger emergency fund to reduce the waiting period cost.*

4) Age and Health: The older or less healthy you are, the more expensive it will be. So, when buying disability insurance, it will never be as cheap than what it costs today.

5) Occupation: The risker your profession is, the more expensive it will be (ex: Stuntman). Good thing, optometry is considered a fairly low-risk profession. You can't really die from doing refraction.

These main five factors set up the ***Base Price*** for typical LTD coverage for a few years, resulting in only a **1% cost of your annual salary per year in premiums**. But if you want additional and fuller protection with a longer benefit period, you might be paying close to ***3% of your annual salary per year in premiums***. There are a lot of extra features are called RIDERS that you can add to your policy, but will come at extra fees.

Example of Extra Features/Riders:

1) Non-Cancellable Option: Your insurance company cannot cancel your policy or raise your premium rate if you switch your job to pursue another passion like professional skydiving.

2) Own Occupation Policy: You are still able to collect disability benefits if you are too disabled to return to being an optometrist but can do another kind of work like Internet blogger. This is different from an **"any occupation" policy**, which only pay your benefits if you are too disabled to do any kind of work at all.

3) Student Loan Rider: Allow you to get additional coverage to pay off student loan balances while disabled. This is important for people who might refinance to a private lender, therefore will not be able to reap the benefits of federal loan forgiveness in an event of disability.

4) Future Purchase Option: Allow you to increase your coverage in the future without providing additional medical insurability. This is great for young doctors who expect their income to increase in the future.

5) Partial or Residual Disability Benefits: Pay a benefit even if you are still working part time as an Optometrist but experience a significant loss of income (less hours worked or reduced productivity) due to injury.

There are many other types of riders that different insurance companies offer. While these options are great and able to be customized to your specific personal situation, *it is clear that you don't need all types of riders*. It is important to speak with a disability insurance agent/broker to make sure you have all the protection you need.

What about Short-term Disability Insurance (STD)?

Short-term disability insurance (STD) basically replaces your income for a short period (3-6 months). STD can essentially cover that waiting period before your long-term disability kicks in. Some female doctors can also get a short-term disability policy that specifically covers future planned pregnancies. But for the mass majority of us, simply having a large enough emergency fund of 6 months will be enough to cover any brief time of no income.

(4) Long Term Life Insurance:

Life insurance is one of those situations that no one wants to address or even think about because frankly, it is quite morbid. If you are single and have nobody that depends on your income (ex: Elderly parents, spouse or children), then to be honest, *you don't really need life insurance.*

For the mass majority of doctors with family or people who depends on your income, it is wise to consider what financial consequences your death can have on the people you leave behind. Simply, to have that peace of mind knowing that your family will be provided for financially upon your passing is extremely comforting.

How Much Life Insurance should I get?

There are a few basic guidelines to help doctors determine how much term life insurance one should actually get.

Pre-Tax Yearly Salary x 17 = Amount of Term Life Insurance

Example: If an optometrist is the sole income provider for his spouse and children, with an average salary of $120,000. Then, he would just need to purchase roughly $2 million worth of life insurance ($120,000 x 17). With this amount of coverage, his wife should be able to replace all of his income with the yearly interest earned by properly investing the $2 million in low cost stock/bonds diverse index fund.

How does this work? Assuming conservative average yearly return of 7%, the yearly gain will *be roughly $140,000* and can be used to support the family, without touching the original principle investment of $2 million.

If your spouse can work halftime after your death and your family only relies on half of your doctor's salary for their expenses, then you *may only need 5-10X* your salary in your life insurance.

The whole goal of life insurance is to maintain your family's comfort of livings.

How Much Life Insurance Can I Afford and for Long?

Term life insurance is relatively cheap but shouldn't be exceed your monthly budget. If your life insurance will lapse if you miss any single payment so make sure it is within your budget so you can make the payments! You should ONLY get enough term life insurance to last you until you are retired (assuming your retirement nest egg will be enough) or financially independent, *whichever happens first*. Another reason is because life insurance will be more expensive as you get older since you are more likely to die and give a payout (Duh right?)

Example: Assuming you are a 35-year-old optometrist in great health making $170,000 salary, you can sign up for 30-year Fixed rate with a 3 million coverage for roughly $2370 a year (or $197 monthly payment). If something suddenly happens to you, your family will be fully protected until your retirement account kicks in.

If you choose a shorter term like 15 years, that is perfectly fine as well. It will be more affordable compared to the 30 years term. After 15 years expiration, you can choose to renew it for another 10 or 15 years but risk paying the higher premium due to your older age risk.

But many doctors at this time might be financially free and therefore do not need any life insurance to support their family.

> *As a General Guideline, we recommend 15 years Fixed Term as an Initial Choice for Life Insurance*

Who should I buy Life Insurance For?

It boggles my mind when I see doctor buy life insurance for their children. WHY?? You are not relying on your children for any income so basically you are betting to make money if they ever die, which is morbid as heck. *Life insurance should only be purchased to replace the potential income loss in case of a death.*

So, aside from buying life insurance for the primary income provider, one should also buy life insurance for the non-working spouse as well. If your spouse is a stay-at-home husband or wife, calculate how much life insurance you should get to replace her "income" to maintain the household like cost of hiring a full time nanny to take care of the kids until they are 18 years old. This is somewhat tricky since it is variable but it is always better on err on the higher side.

What about Whole Life Insurance?

Very few things in life get me pissed off and whole life insurance is one of them. This is probably **one of the biggest financial scams** that many insurance salesmen will use to prey on "smart" doctors, and will go by many names such as **Universal, Universal index, Variable or Permanent life insurance**. Whole life insurance is sold to provide life insurance coverage, as well as a cash value policy that is supposed to be invested and promoted to grow tax-free. *Sounds good right? NOPE!*

Three Reasons Why Whole Life Insurance is a Rip-off:

1) Fees are too high and costly:

- Whole life insurance has a ridiculously high monthly premium payment and *is almost 22x* the amount of a cheap term life.

2) Poor Return on Investment for Cash Value Policy:

- The whole life insurance itself has extreme low returns, roughly 2-3% but only after having the policy for over 15 years. RIDICULOUS RIGHT? This is not even beating the yearly inflation rate of 3-4%. Many of the time, the policy will have a negative return due to heavy up-front sale commission fee and high surrender fee (what you pay to quit the policy early). In many cases after 10-15 years, you either break even or lose money.

3) You don't need the income Tax or Estate Tax benefits:

- Many salesmen will be quick to point out that loans can be taken from the cash policy tax-free and better than your 401K or IRA account. *No Shit, Einstein,* it should be tax-free if you using post-tax money to pay the premium to fund this cash policy.

- Another "tax benefit" that most salesmen will try to promote is death benefit of the policy to help "wealthy" optometrist avoid estate taxes. But under current law, a couple doesn't even have to start paying estate taxes until they have a *net worth of 10 million*, a figure that many Optometrists won't reach in their lifetime.

The simple take-away is to **AVOID** *whole life insurance at all cost,* don't be one of those dumb doctors that get preyed on by insurance salesman posting as a financial advisor. If your financial advisor even remotely brings whole life insurance, **FIRE HIS ASS!** Buy cheap Term Life insurance and use any of the ridiculously high whole life monthly payments to invest in your own tax-efficient retirement accounts such as your 401K, Roth IRA and other IRAs, then dump the rest in a taxable brokerage account (15% long term Capital gain tax). This will give you better cash liquidity and mimic the S&P 500 Stock Index average return of 10-12%.

Eff my Life, What if I already signed up for Whole Life Insurance?

If you already fell prey to one when you were a naïve young doctor, sorry to hear that! **But yes, dump it, eat the high cost surrender fees and let it be a very expensive life lesson....** The only time that I would even consider keeping a whole life insurance is if you had it for greater than 15 years (usually as a gift inheritance from your parents), then you can compare the total cost of surrendering the policy versus paying future premiums into it. *99% of the time, it is better to dump it.*

Remember a pig dressed in makeup is still a pig, that is what is basically what whole life insurance is.

(5) What about Car Insurance?

Car insurance is pretty straightforward since it is against the law to drive around uninsured. Most states require a minimum liability coverage. Here are some car insurance coverage's that you can get:

1) Liability coverage: If you are responsible for the car accident, then it will *cover only cover the other party's injuries or property damage caused in the collision.* Most States require a minimum amount of coverage

2) Collision Coverage: Covers the cost to *repair or replace your own car* if it is damaged or destroyed in a wreck.

3) Comprehensive Coverage: Additional insurance that covers any damages that aren't caused by a car wreck, such as theft, vandalism, fire, hail, etc.

The most important thing is just to make sure you carry enough liability insurance. Although many states only require you to carry a minimum of $50,000, that is usually not enough. If you accidentally hit and severely injure a person in their brand new Lexus, their Lexus repair and medical bills alone will be significantly costly and can go upwards in the hundreds of thousands dollars.

For collision and comprehensive coverage, it is entirely up to you and frankly doesn't matter. If you drive a $2,000 value old car and have enough cash in your emergency fund to replace it in case of an accident, then you don't need collision or comprehensive coverage. If you drive a brand new Mercedes and replacing your car would be financially devastating, then get enough coverage collision insurance to cover the car replacement.

A little side note, if you don't have the funds to afford a brand-new car in case of an emergency, then you should not be driving it.

(6) What about House or Renter's Insurance?

Homeowner's insurance is one of the most important coverage to get mainly because your house is such a significant financial asset in our portfolio. It is basically property insurance that covers losses and damages to the house itself and any assets within the home. Many insurances will have a deductible requirement on the claim, which means the owner will have to pay any out of pocket expenses until a certain limit before the insurance cover the rest.

Example: If the home deductible limit is $4,000, and your living room burned down causing a claim payment of $15,000. The insurance company will only pay $11,000, once you met your deductible. Similar to health insurance, the higher your deductible is, the lower your monthly premium payment will be.

There are 4 basic type of coverage when it comes to Homeowner insurances:

1) Dwelling Coverage: Insure the actual structure of the house and other building attachment (like garages) and built-in appliances (like water heater).

2) Personal Property Coverage: Insure your personal possessions such as furniture's, laptops, clothing's, etc.

3) Liability coverage: Insure you against lawsuits that may be filed against you if someone is injured on your property. Example, if your dog bites the mailman.

4) Additional living expenses (ALE) coverage: Covers the cost of temporary housing (such as hotel) if your house becomes uninhabitable due to covered damage.

(7) What about Umbrella Insurance?

The last insurance policy that some doctors can get is umbrella coverage. It is basically a *last-resort extra layer of protection* for you and any one of your assets. This is when your insurance coverage exceeds the limit amount of your typical policies like home insurance, malpractice, health insurance, etc.

Example: If you purchase $1 million dollars umbrella policy, and you are involved in a several multiple car collisions in which *you are at fault.* The total damage can include multiple cars destructions, property damage, heavy medical bills, personal emotional lawsuits, etc. This can add up quite quickly, and let say will have a total at-fault liability cost of $800,000. If your auto insurance liability only cover up to the $50,000 limit, then you are screwed!

After that $50,000 is paid by your auto insurance, you will be personally sued for additional compensations of the remaining $750,000. This will expose your saving/home and future wage earnings, leading to personal bankruptcy.

But if you were a financially prepared doctor and read this book, and you wisely signed up for a *$1 million dollars umbrella policy,* then the policy will pick up the rest of the $750,000, up to a $1 million, saving you from bankruptcy! Whew! Close call!

How much Umbrella Insurance should a doctor get?

Usually a standard policy from $500,000 to $1.5 million is often enough. The yearly cost of an umbrella policy is fairly low due to its low risk, ranging in fees from $400-500 a year for a $1 million dollars policy. It is definitely worth that much for peace of mind.

In summary, insurance is one of those adult things that is not the most exciting thing in the world but is *so freaking important.* Many doctors, especially young ones, will often defer getting the necessary insurances until it is often too late. Remember, you are often just *one bad day away from bankruptcy.*

A good rule when it comes to insurance coverage is to prepare for the worst catastrophic events that will financially devastate your life and career. You do NOT have to get every single insurance policy out there with every single add-on rider out there! You don't need to be getting insurance warranty on that iPhone. Yes, it will suck if your iPhone is broken but it won't financially bankrupt you. That is what having a decent size emergency fund is for.

Okay that is it! You are a BEAST for getting through this boring chapter. Go have a beer!

The Optometrist's Guide to Financial Freedom

CHAPTER 13:When to get Expert Help BY: Dat

"Just realize that just because you are a do-it-yourselfer, does not mean that you need to be a rabid DIY-er. You can always get financial advice a la carter"

-Jim Dahle, M.D.

When we were writing this book, Aaron and I kept one mission in mind and that is to teach you the fundamental of personal finance that any typical optometrist can handle.

While we are both big advocate of do-it-yourself when it comes to investing and other areas of finance, we do realize the importance of professional help when needed. It is similar to knowing your own strengths and weakness as a doctor.

I personally love ocular disease and can handle almost anything that comes through my exam door. But when it comes to binocular vision therapy, whew! No thanks! I will gladly refer that out ASAP without a moment's hesitation. It might be a combination of my limited knowledge or lack of interest in binocular vision, but I know that it isn't my strong suit.

But as a general optometrist, I am still required to know the fundamentals of how binocular vision therapy works so I can make the necessary referrals to a specific doctor, and simply not look like an idiot when talking to my patient.

The same can be applied to personal finance. As we accumulate more wealth as doctors, knowing which areas you are comfortable managing yourself and which areas you want to refer to the professionals is vital. Here are 4 main types of professional that an OD might need in his financial life and career:

1. **Tax Professional***
2. **Financial advisor** *
3. **Real Estate Professional**
4. **Insurance Broker**

But the two professionals that we will primarily focus on in this chapter are tax accountant and financial advisor. *Why?* Both fields will significantly impact your wealth building as an OD

Section 1: Do I need a Tax Professional?

Okay, let face it. Taxes are one of the most boring things out there. I dare to even say it is worse than trying to memorize all the different ray-tracing diagrams of optometric optics, *a complete snooze-fest.* Heck, I am even yawning as I am writing this section! Our tax system is unnecessary complex, full of regulations and ever-changing tax codes (Thanks IRS!). It isn't even a question of if you need a tax accountant, *but when...*

For the majority of ODs who are simply W2 employed or 1099 independent contractor and don't have outside business interests like rental or practice ownership, then a software tax program like TurboTax is sufficient enough.

All you must do it to just follow the instructions of the tax program and know what items you can deduct as an optometrist, especially in a 1099 income tax situation.

What are some Tax Deductions that you can make as an Optometrist?

So, your goal during tax season is to reduce your marginal taxable gross income so you can play fewer taxes, regardless if you are W2 employee or 1099 independent contractor

(1) Tax-Deferred Retirement Plans.

This is the largest tax deduction that a lot of optometrist misses out on. Every single dollar that you put in your tax-deferred retirement account will *not be taxed on* for that year.

So, if you are a W2 employee with an employer-sponsored 401K, you should be contributing $19,000 a year (as of 2019) and doing a Roth IRA ($6,000, backdoor if you are above the income limit). Even though the Roth IRA won't give you a tax break, it will still protect your retirement investment from future taxes!

If you're an independent contractor (paid on 1099 income) you should be able to contribute 25% of your income to a SEP-IRA, up to a maximum of $56,000, with an additional "catch-up" contribution of $6,000 if you're over 50. Heck, if you own your own practice or work in a practice that have a profit-sharing (PSP) or defined benefit plan (DBP), you can shelter even more!

(2) Health Care

If you own your own business or pay yourself as a 1099 independent, you can actually deduct your monthly health insurance premiums since you don't have an employer to pay for your health care.

In addition, if you have a high deductible medical plan, you can contribute to a Health Saving account or HSA ($3,500 Single, Family $7,000 and Additional Catch up $1,000 for greater than 55 years old).

As discussed in the previous retirement chapter, this is **triple-tax advantaged** since you can first fund it with pre-tax dollars, and secondly can use it for any health-care expenses (without tax paid or 10% early withdrawal penalty). Lastly, HSA can act as additional retirement vehicle, which is similar to a Roth IRA, since there are no taxes on growth but you can withdraw any funds without penalty after 65 year old for anything you desire.

(3) Mortgage Interest

As you already know, if you own a home, you can *deduct the interest* on acquisition indebtedness, basically whatever your mortgage is used to buy, build or improve your home up to $750,000. So, while I do not advocate this strategy at all, you technically take out a home equity line of credit (HELOC) loan, which you can use to pay off any other debts like high interest credit card or student loans. This loan would increase your mortgage amount, which would cost you more in interest, allowing you to deduct more in tax.

So, do we advise this route? Heck no, it is never a good idea to use your house as an ATM!

(4) Charity

Optometrists tend to be the most charitable profession compared to most people since most of us got into the field to help people. For any donation gift, *any amount up to $250 will only require a receipt or cancelled check*. For gifts of property such as clothes and supplies valuing up to $500, you need to have a receipt listing the organization, date of donation and a description of the items and its value. Anything above the $250 cash + $500 Items limit, will require a written acknowledgement and an appraisal.

If you volunteer a lot with a charitable program such as giving away your optometric services, you can always deduct any miles that you travel to the site, along with any expenses associated with your donating your time. Unfortunately, you can't just deduct a value for the time you spent volunteering.

(5) Business Expenses

If you are a self-employed doctor (1099 income) or private practice owner, there is a whole world of tax deductions that you can take advantage of! Just make sure you keep careful record of your business expenses in case of a possible future audit.

Examples:

- Continuing Education Costs such as hotel/flights/convention fees/meals

- Optometry Medical License/DEA License

- Professional society dues (AOA, local society dues)

- Interest paid student loans only if your adjusted gross income is less than <$80,000 Single or <165,000 Married. *Sadly, most doctors will not qualify for this tax break unless they are part time or usually their first year out.*

- Professional Fees such as legal, accounting/tax, financial planner

- Payroll for employees

- Lab Coats/Scrubs/uniform with dry cleaning fee

- Newly purchased Optometric equipment such as BIO, trial lens, etc.

- Large equipment purchases such as OCT, Retina Optos, etc.

- Books/magazines such as medical journals and periodicals

- Pager/Cell Phone

- Office Supplies/ Medical Supplies such as computer software, and ancillary equipment

- Vehicles, Business travel for CE/Conventions+ commuting between offices (Caution)

- Meals and entertainment (Caution)

- Office meetings and parties (Caution)

What can I deduct as a W2 Employee?

W2 employed doctors are *extremely limited in their tax deductions*, since it is expected that their employer will pay and cover most of their business expenses/equipment.

So how can one get around this? First, try to convince your employer to pay for any mandatory expenses that you might need as an optometrist such as license renewal, DEA license, professional membership payments, CE classes allowance, etc. This way, your expenses got covered and your employer gets to pay them with pre-tax dollars.

This is even more tax-effective if you have other 1099 income from other fill-in optometry offices. Even though 90% of your total yearly income comes for your main W2 optometry full time job, this doesn't mean that you cannot deduct all the SAME job expenses required for you to do your 1099 optometry fill-in. If the moonlighting 1099 job requires you to have an optometry license, DEA license, and having continuing education classes, then you can deduct your business expenses from that 1099 income! Provided that you have a receipt for the purchase and your W2 employer reimburse you. This is truly a *Win WIN situation!*

(6) Tax Harvesting

This is a little bit more complicated but if you have a taxable brokerage account via Vanguard or Fidelity, you can get a little break on your taxes (up to $3,000 per year in investment losses) at the end of the year if you experience a significant loss in your portfolio. How?

By SELLING YOUR LOSER and BUYING A SIMILAR FUND.

For example, if I brought $100,000 worth of Vanguard S&P 500 index fund initially for 2018 and I lost $3000 that year since the market was bad for 2018. If I sold the $100,000 with a loss of $3,000, I can "harvest" up to $3,000 in tax deduction by buying $100,000 of another similar fund such as Vanguard Total Stock Market index. So, if 2019 is a good year, and that $100,000 produce $10,000 in gain, then I can deduct that $3,000 "harvest" toward that $10,000 profit. But the 15% long-term capital tax would still apply to the $7,000 gain profit.

Even though these two funds are different, they are highly correlated to each other in the market since both funds invest in the overall stock market and have the similar varying return. Other examples can be Fidelity REIT with Schwab REIT or Russell 2000 Value Index with Vanguard Small Cap 600 Value Index.

One last caution, be aware of the **30 Days Wash-sale Rule** which mean you cannot buy back what you just sold (including your spouse) nor can you sell the shares you just brought within 30 days!

Who really needs to hire a Tax Accountant?

1) Owner of a S-Corporation, LLC or Partnership, Private practice owner or sublease holder

2) High-income Earner: If you make over $200,000 or have a net worth of over $1 million, you are 4x more likely to be audited especially if you are self-preparing.

3) Outside investments such as real estate rental, passive income like side business, taxable brokerage investing account where you want to take advantages of gains/losses tax harvesting

4) Self-Employed contractor (like 1099): If you are not comfortable doing your own tax deductions

What are the Two Main Types of Tax Accountant?

While there is an alphabet soup of license designation, the only two meaningful ones are Public Accountant (CPA) and Tax Enrolled Agents (EAs). The difference is that CPA is significantly more trained (and thus more expensive) and has a qualified license by passing an extremely difficult test and having to maintain yearly CE courses. An

EA can be sufficient in doing your taxes as well but some might be more knowledgeable depending on their training.

Once you decide that you need professional help, **here are 3 tips on finding a good accountant to work with.**

1) Referrals from Healthcare professionals: Chat with your professional friends and see if they like working with their own CPAs

2) Check out the firm's website: See if they have experience working with other optometrists

3) Interview with the tax accountant:

- Many accountant firms will allow you to come in for a free consult to get them to know them in person to see if you two are a good fit. Many firms will do via videoconference, in person or via phone.
- Some questions to ask:
    - *Why do you think I need a CPA and what are some something you can offer that I cannot do myself?*
    - *What are your experiences working with healthcare professionals like myself?*
    - *Can you give me estimated cost on what I expect from using your service? And will you be using a Fixed Price Agreement (FPA)?*
        - **Note:** FPA is basically all-inclusive, one-year fixed cost for all services.
    - *Any financial relationship with other business that you might be referring me to use?*

Remember that a great tax accountant can be worth their weight in gold especially if your taxes are complex. But for the majority of doctors, their tax situation is honestly isn't that complicated and can often be managed by themselves. Overall, you want a tax accountant that is really detailed, resourceful, proactive and finally teach you through the process.

Section 2: Do I need a Financial Advisor?

By now at the end of this book, you should realize that we are big advocate of Do-It-Yourself investing. Simply by reading this book, you are significantly more financially knowledgeable than 95% of your fellow optometrists! Heck! You probably know just as much as certified financial planner (CFA), if not more. We are aware that not every doctor wants to manage his or her money, either due to time or simply lack of interest, so hiring an advisor is perfectly fine!

We would much rather have optometrists start investing sooner and pay a fee for help, then *not invest at all.* With that being said, for the remainder of this section, we will try convincing you on why you do NOT need a financial advisor. Then if you do decide to seek out professional help, we will help you seek a financial advisor that is right for you. *Regardless, you should ALWAYS have a general basic knowledge of how investing works.*

Four Reasons why you do NOT need a Financial Advisor:

1) You will save a Crap-load of Money

Any professional financial advice is expensive, especially if you are paying an asset-under-management (AUM) advisory fee in which the financial advisor will **automatically take 1-3% of your portfolio each year**, REGARDLESS, if your portfolio made money that year or not. Consequently, even for 2008 Recession where many investors lost 30-40% of their money in their IRA, those with financial advisors lost *even more.* Remember that financial advisors will always make money no matter what the market outcome is.

You might be asking yourself, wait it is just 1%? Why is that such a big deal?

Well that 1% over a lifetime of investing can end up costing you hundreds of thousands in advisory fees.

Example: Let compare two typical 26-year-old newly graduated optometrist: Smart Sammy and Lazy Larry. Both have $25,000 in their IRA retirement and add $10,000 each year to his account each year. Let assume a typical 7% average annual return, both plan to retire in 40 years. Let examine the effects of DIY investing *versus* using a 1% Financial Advisory fee.

Scenario 1: Smart Sammy decides to do it himself and invest in a cheap, low cost index fund with Vanguard. After 40 years, his net returns for retirement is **roughly $2,500,000.** Damn baby! that is a lot of cheese! Woot!

Scenario 2: Lazy Larry decides, *"Psh, it is just 1% fee"* and hires a financial advisor. Assuming the advisor does the ethical thing and put him in the same cheap index fund. After 40 years, his net returns for retirement is **roughly $1,910,000**, *resulting in a $590,000 fee* in sacrificed return toward his financial advisor.

Shocking right?? That is close to *$14,750 in advisory fee you paid each year* over 40 years of investing! All for some greedy bastard to put you in a simple index fund.

That is not the worst part of it! The financial advisor needs to somehow justify his professional fee, so he is going to overcomplicate your portfolio with expensive front-loaded mutual funds (5% purchasing cost) or even worse, actively managed mutual funds (higher expense ratio cost of 1-2%, compared to a typical S&P 500 Index fund with only expense ratio of 0.02%). This means if we include the financial advisory fee of 1-3% with the costs of their loaded or actively managed funds choice (1-5%).

This means that some portfolio assets under management's overall cost can be as *high as 6%!*

What if my financial advisor can bring in a higher advertised actively managed return compared to the market's passive index return, is it okay to pay a higher commission fee?

It is extremely difficult to beat the return of a passive, low cost index fund that mirrors the overall market's return. An actively managed fund might do better in some years, but over a course of 10-20 years investing, after accounting for advisory, trading fees, and mutual funds fees, *an index fund will almost always win.*

There was a famous 10-year bet that the most successful investor of our generation Warren Buffet made against actively managed Hedge Funds back in 2007. He bet $1 Million that a *simple low cost S&P 500 index fund would outperform the performance of basket of multiple group of hedge funds* at the end of 2017. The hedge funds can select any fund they want to actively manage but will need to subtract their commission fee at the end to get the *true net return.* All proceeds will go to charity.

The results? NOT EVEN CLOSE.

At the end of 2017, **Buffet's S&P 500 index fund return 7.1%,** while the competing basket of stocks and funds selected by professional asset managers returned only a minuscule **average of 2.2%,** not even beating the rate of inflation.

The lesson here is *fee matters a lot* and investors need to be aware of it. A lot of doctors are worried that they won't do as good as a professional financial advisor. But bear in mind that you don't even have to do as well as the advisor, you just need to do as well as the advisor *minus his fee,* and that is extremely easier to beat!

2) You can Learn everything your Own-self

Aaron and I always get this question, *"How the heck you guys know so much about finances and investing?"* Simple, it literally took us one week to learn the basic fundamentals by picking up a few personal finances/investing books and BOOM that's it. Compared to all the crazy ocular diseases that we had to memorize back in school, it was truthfully a piece of cake to understand.

There is not much to learn or much needed strict discipline required to *be our own financial advisor and investment manager.* Heck, Aaron and I were able to achieve a significant net worth within 5-10 years of graduation by simply reading a few books, browsing a few blog websites, goggling a few terms, and listening to a few podcasts. That was it! We had our basic financial game plan and investing foundation.

Advisors will try to convince you that you need their services by stating that there are a lot of complicated things in personal finance and investing such as the difference IBR vs REPAYE student loan repayment plans, 401K vs defined benefits retirement plan, backdoor Roth IRA, tax code, ETF vs front-loaded mutual funds, trust and asset protections etc.

Yes, *while investing and tax can be overly complicated*, close to 90% honestly do not apply to the typical optometrist! You only have to learn about the topic that is affecting your life at the current moment!

If you are a new graduate with $250,000 in student debts, *learn the different types of programs and strategies on how to attack the massive student debt.* Once you are done learning about that topic and want to learn how to invest for wealth building, *pick up an investing book and learn how to analyze a stock.* Fast forward to your retirement and you want to learn about social security and what time is right to withdraw from your accounts? *Then read about social security and required minimum distributions!*

Remember! You only have to learn about the issues that are pertinent to your own financial situation at the moment. Then if you really need professional help or need a 2nd opinion, then hire specialized advice as needed.

Will you make few mistakes?

Sure! But they will be innocent ones at the beginning and you will have the valuable direct lessons of *never making that mistake ever again.* If you start early on, you are just investing with a smaller amount of money, which means that it is better for you to make those dumb mistakes without losing much money.

But with passing each year, you will become a better investor and avoid those newbie pitfalls and sidestep significant damage to your larger asset portfolio. It is like having an optometry license, once you get the fundamentals of knowing how to treat your patients; it is as simple as *"1 or 2, which is clearer?"* But similar to our license and continuing education classes, our financial knowledge base needs to be refreshed every year, with any new tax laws or retirement contribution limits.

3) You won't Screw your own self over

It is extremely fun and exciting to manage your own money! It is like a game, where each year, you can physically see the progress of your investment and see your net worth slowly grow! Finally, there is no one that *is more motivated* to make you the most money than yourself! Which means you cannot rip yourself off by going *"Bernie Madoff"* on your own portfolio. You will not succumb to getting taken advantage by some shady financial advisors.

4) You will pay more Attention to your Finances and Make fewer Mistakes

The greatest benefit of being your own advisor is that you are solely responsible for your financial destiny. Knowing this will cause many doctors to pay more attention to their investment, spending and screen for any mistakes with a more detailed eye.

Also, many investors with a financial advisor will say, *"Oh! My advisors keep me from doing something stupid!"* While I do agree with that statement, but heck your advisor has to do whatever you decide, so if you really want to sell during a crash, no advisors is going to stop you!

Even then, even the most experienced advisors are not immune from trying to chase the next big IPO start up, trying to time the market by doing excessive trading (and thus, accumulating large trading fees, which they transfer the cost over to you) or panicking during a market crash, despite a well-established game plan. They are human just like us but at least with us, *we are aware of our own weakness, strengths and emotions*. Thus, we can adjust our risk tolerance within our portfolio strategies.

How to hire the "Perfect" Advisor?

After reading the previous section, you are still like *"Screw it Dat and Aaron, I really don't want to manage my own finances, can I just hire someone to take care of it!"*

No worries, we are both well aware that some doctors need a little bit more handholding compared to others, so we would much rather have a young doctor start investing paying a small fee, *versus* not investing at all. **Here are six factors to consider when hiring the "perfect" financial advisor**

(1) Fairly Priced, Fee-only advisory

First of all, I would *avoid* assets under managements (AUM) in which a financial advisor will charge 1-2% of your total assets under their management each year, regardless of whether you made a profit or not. This can get ridiculously expensive as your portfolio grows throughout your life! It doesn't require a financial advisor 10X the amount of work to manage your $500,000 portfolio with a 1% fee of

$5,000 yearly, compared to a later $5 Million portfolio with a 1% fee of $50,000 yearly.

Secondly, he will have a natural bias against recommending other financial strategies that make more sense for your life such as paying off your massive debt student/house mortgage, investing in real estate or other side hustles.

Why? *Because the advisor cannot collect a fee on other investments that he is not managing!*

Ideally, if you need professional advice, I would recommend ***an hourly fee-only advisory***, which the FA help you to establish a solid financial plan each year (while managing the asset yourself), and any additional help as needed. Many *fee-only hourly rate can range from $100- $500.*

If you truly want a more hands-off method and want all your assets under management, I would negotiate for ***a flat annual fee rate within the $1,000-$8,000 range per year***, with ***a fee-only hourly rate as needed for additional financial planning.***

(2) Fiduciary Duty and up-to-date Academic Understanding

Like the Hippocratic oath that we took as doctors, we need to find an advisor who upholds a strict fiduciary and ethical obligation to act solely in their client's best financial interest. Also, it goes without saying, you want a financial advisor who is the most up-to-dated on academic concepts, new tax codes and strives to take continuing education to expand their knowledge base.

I am always constantly shocked when I talk to optometrists in our group whose financial advisors don't know about the backdoor Roth IRA. This should be a vital component of any high-income professional's investment plan.

(3) Professional Designations

Your advisors should have at least one or more of the following certifications:
- **Certified Financial Planner** (CFP)

- **Chartered Financial Consultant** (ChFC)
- **Chartered Financial Analyst** (CFA)
- **Certified Public Accountants with Personal Financial Specialist** (CPA/PFS)

If my advisor is helping me with financial planning, it is recommended that he or she should have at least one of these designations. If he is helping me manage my investments, then he better have a CFA. This shows that the advisor is committed to his field and went through the minimal education and examination certification to be licensed within his field. If your advisor doesn't have any of these designations, then he likely doesn't know much more than you at this point of the book.

(4) Similar Clienteles

The perfect advisor should know all the specific financial situations that a high-income earning doctor will face such as how to tackle their student loan; whether the OD should do 10-year Public Service Loan Forgiveness if they are working in a VA or refinance their student loan for a lower rate. Other topics can include how to do backdoor Roth IRA, private practice business loan, etc. *The list goes on and on.* Thus, it is highly recommended that you find an advisor that has a history of working with optometrists.

(5) Able to provide other Professional Services

You might have heard from your fellow co-workers, "Oh! I have a money guy who handles all my investments!" The truth is that many financial advisor *can only do 2 or 3 things really well such as financial planning, and/or investment management,* but he should able to have a team to support him for other areas such as insurance agent, estate attorney, retirement consultant, tax accountant, contract/business negotiator, etc. You want a financial advisor who has a well-run team to support you in all area of your financial life and work seamlessly together.

(6) Investing Strategies

Ideally, your investing personality should match your financial advisor's personality and approach to investing. If you are conservative, you won't work well with an advisor who takes on risky investments.

While every single advisor invests a little different, his strategy should be reasonable and have low fees in mind. He should have a mixture of low-cost mutual funds like the S&P 500 index, along with some mixture of low-cost ETFs/Sector ETFs to get exposed to certain areas like tech if that sector is profitable that year, or even do some active trading based on recent events or market momentum. He might even introduce some commercial real estate or even private loans to business. Whatever his strategy might be, it should be reasonable, low cost and easy for you to understand.

So, what are some red flags that you should be cautious about when looking at your financial advisor's portfolio:

- **1) Recommending whole life insurance** or other similar insurance like index/universal. This is an insurance salesman masking as a FA, Run away quickly!

- **2) Picking high-risk and volatile individual stocks or "Hype" investments** like weed stock or Bitcoin.

- **3) High frequency rate of trading.** Remember that any additional fees will be charged to you.

- **4) Choosing actively managed funds, front/back loaded funds,** which might cost an additional 3-5% fee to purchase that fund.

- **5) Being too complicated!** Remember that a simple three-funds investing can be successful, if not more, than the most complex funds. If you see 20 different assets or funds in your portfolio, the advisor is likely trying to overwhelm you and is likely trying to convince that *his high fee cost is justified by how complex your portfolio is.*

211

Now that you are aware of all the pros and cons of whether a financial advisor offer, you can decide for yourself whether one is right for you or not. Honestly, by you simply picking up this book, you are probably more than knowledgeable enough to manage your own finances and don't need a FA to hold your hands.

With that being said, Aaron and I completely get that certain doctors don't have the time or even the interest to manage their own finances, so in that case, a ***good financial advisor at a reasonable price*** is better than not investing at all.

CHAPTER 14: How to Create a Side Hustle BY: Dat

"Residual income is passive income that comes in every month whether you show up or not. It is when you don't get paid on your personal efforts alone, but you get paid on the efforts of hundreds or even thousands of other and on the efforts of your money! It is one of the keys to financial freedom and time freedom"

– Steve Fisher

With the increasing burden of massive student debt and low vision plan insurance reimbursement rate, many optometrists are searching for income alternative to make extra money aside from their full-time optometric profession. Many optometrists are looking for ways (either passive or active) to supplement or even completely replacing their current income by doing "side hustle".

So why do you need a side hustle? To be honest, you don't. Simply being a full-time optometrist will provide a steady income to be financially successful. But having a side hustle will increase your total income and help you achieve financial freedom quicker and accomplish other financial goals. More importantly, many ODs start a side hustle because it is something that they truly enjoy and are

213

passionate about. It is often a way to keep things fresh from the repetitive nature of optometry at times.

There is a famous statistic that millionaires usually will have an average of **SEVEN streams of income,** whether they are active or passive. So, I think we as ODs can strive for least 5 streams. So, what is the difference between active and passive?

Active Income: When you work majority of the time and are paid for your expertise and time. This usually requires actual hours and physically being there. This is basically you seeing patients at your optometry office.

Passive Income: When the payment is not directly tied to you working or being there. Don't mistake passive income with zero work; it will often require a significant amount of active work and long hours at the beginning before it can truly produce cash flow without you being there all the time.

- Some examples can include investment dividends, rental properties, or even for example, royalty from this book. (*HAHA trust us, Aaron and I don't make much from creating this book*).

What are Some Tips for starting your Side Hustle?

First of all, don't ever quit your day job.

Unless you inherit a million dollars from your rich uncle, you are likely starting without any fund or resources. Being an optometrist is an extremely lucrative profession and should be your primary source of active income, *at least for now.* Keep on working your day job until you saved enough cash to start your side hustle. You can easily do it by both SAVING MORE (aka Frugal living) and EARNING MORE (working extra fill-in OD shifts during your days off).

Second, *seek Passion over Profit.*

Start with finding your passion or area of interest. Having a business idea that you are truly passionate is a great indication for future success. Side hustles take a lot work and time, but it doesn't have to feel like a job. If your side-hustle is something you are passionate about, it will motivate you to work that extra 2-3 hours late at night after you are exhausted from a long day of refracting patients or miss out on that raging party in the city with your buddies. Passion creates energy, and it is that energy that drives you to succeed.

Third, brainstorm a crap-load of ideas and write them down!

No matter how ridiculous it might sound. Start with asking your friends and family on what they think you are most exceptional at, whether it might be creative drawing, building wooden tables, giving good advice, or having a great specific personality trait. Start with your strengths first and use that in forming your ideas. This will make it easier to execute down the line. Even if something is an amazing idea but you can't imagine yourself executing it, then it is a *Moo-point*, you know a cow's opinion, it just doesn't' matter (HaHa 90's pop culture TV reference for all you Friends Fans out there).

Fourth, *be Strategic and know that Execution is key.*

There are many stories of companies with amazing ideas, which eventually collapse due to poor leadership or awful business plan. One perfect example was WebVan.com back in the 1990s, which was an online E-commerce store where consumer could have groceries and household items delivered straight to their door. Sounds Familiar? You are probably thinking to yourself, *"Wait, isn't that what CEO Jeff Bezos of Amazon is doing now?"* It was basically the same great idea as Amazon but due to poor management and execution, WebVan.com went bankrupt.

Once you have a set idea, you need to have a set and logical business plan that makes sense. Lay out a frame-wire on how you will make money, which market or niche will this work in? Who is your biggest competition? How much money will you need to get it started? What are your goals each year? And then, *analyze the HECK out of it.* List all the reasonable things that can do right or wrong with your side hustle. Then finally have someone else take a look at it with a fresh set of eyes, don't be afraid to take constructive criticism.

Fifth, Trust yourself and be Confident in your ideas.

If you able to talk yourself out of doing your own business idea, then you should not be doing in the first place. But once you established your mindset, be confident in your ideas and stick with it! Don't count on others to give you validation when attempting something new.

The most successful business ideas out there are ones that push the boundaries of what is traditionally view as "safe" or "possible". Take Uber for example, there were so many critics in the early stages saying it will never work due to legal restrictions and pushback from the cab industry but Uber still persists and it overcame criticism to become one of the most successful disruptions of the taxi industry.

Finally, Always Stay Humble.

There is always room for you as an entrepreneur to learn. Be respectful and always listen before you come to any conclusion. Make sure you take the time out to show gratitude toward people that helped you along the way. This ensures that your side hustle will last for decades to come.

What are some Side Hustle ideas or Passive income for Optometrist?

Ideas Using your Optometric Degree:
- Fill-in optometry Day Diem aside from your full-time job.
- Tele-health at the VA Site (such as monitoring for diabetic retinopathy).
- Vision Screening for clubs and organizations (Many will fundraise money to hire an OD for the day).
- Member on hospital board or on Optometry school board.
- Optometric Consulting for contact lens research, new medical devices, pharmaceuticals and other healthcare companies.
- Optometry content writer for medical journals or optometric publications.
- Expert Medical Witness in legal cases.
- Chart/Utilization patient review (such as for worker's compensation and insurance) or Doctor's options on Medical Cases.
- CE Lectures Speakers or other Speaking engagement.
- Part time clinical instructor or teaching assistant.
- Optometry research for clinical and pharmaceutical trials.
- Optometric-specific Surveys (Online): Ranges $10-$200
  - M3 Global Research
  - MNOW Surveys
- On-Demand Doctor Visits: Heal.com, Pager.com

Ideas using your Medical Knowledge/ Influence
- Write a book, paperback or eBook (Amazon self-publish) on various topics.
- Create online Blog.
- Create online courses (ex: such as KMK NBEO study guide).
- Become an Instagram or other social media Influencer promoting various optometric products or lifestyle.

- Optometric experts on TV, film or radio.
- Podcasting and YouTube video blogging.
- Tutoring.
- Sell Items on Esty.com or eBay.com.
- Direct to consumer products (for example: Selling a specialized home-made product like birdhouse feeders).

Ideas with Real Estate:

- Part time Real Estate License: Selling homes on weekend.
- Rent out your own home via Airbnb.com
- Real Estate Rental homes investing such as apartment, single-family home, and vacations rentals.
- Invest in crowd-funding real estate:
  - Equitymultiple.com, RichUncles.com, Biggerpocket.com, Realtyshares.com
- Invest in tax liens properties.

Ideas in Business

- Create invention or make an existing product better, can be optometric or non-optometric.
- Create a mobile application using sites like ibuildapp.com and buildfire.com.
- Multi-level marketing (MLM): Caution, a lot of these business are scams.
- Angel Investing in new technology or companies (ex: Angellist.com, microventures.com).
- Venture capitalist consultant: consult firms that fund medical innovations, especially in optometry.

Ideas with Investing/Lending

- Day-Trading with the Stock market:
  - Remember this is completely different from mutual funds. Involves extensive investing knowledge about individual stocks and timing the market to try to sell

high/buy low. Involves a significant amount of risk and speculation.
- Peer-to-peer lending: Lendingclub.com, Prosper.com

Miscellaneous Ideas
- Free-lancing any skills, whether it is optometry-related or not.
  - o Examples: www.fiverr.com, www.Upwork.com
- Drive Uber/Lyft during your free time
- Rent out your car
  - o Example: www.Turo.com
- Photography/Wedding gigs/ Photo booth
- Teaching a specific topic class like Yoga, or Taxes 101

Finally, is it actually worth it?

I think all doctors have the smarts and drive to start a side hustle. I mean, *snaps, we made it through 4 grueling years of optometry school.* But not every optometrist has the determination to be entrepreneur, which is completely fine because the optometric profession is a noble one. Most side hustles in the beginning requires a lot of long nights and weekends, therefore limiting the amount of personal time.

At the end of the day, you need to look at your own personal situation and see if it is even worth your time? This is when passion and having the right attitude can often motivate you to keep on going.

Ultimately, like everything in finance, it is personal for a reason; you got to have the right drive and motivation to keep on going.

The Optometrist's Guide to Financial Freedom

CHAPTER 15: Our Philosophy and Final Word of Wisdoms

BY: Dat and Aaron

"An investment in knowledge pays the best interest "
-Benjamin Franklin

Congratulations! You made it to the final chapter! We were debating about how we were going to end this book with a long-winded chapter beautifully expressing word of wisdoms in a life-changing style.

Then we were like *"Screw it"*, we are talking to a bunch of eyeballs nerds who went to Optometry School whose brains from years of studying have gotten so used to seeing everything concise and straight to point in bullet-list format.

So, if you forgot everything that you read here (we know that insurance chapter was a doozy), here are **15 important take-away:**

1. Execution is everything, so create a solid game and take action today!
2. There are many roads to wealth, choose the one that work well for you!
3. Don't invest in shit that you don't understand. If it sounds too good to be true, it is likely a get-rich scam!

4. Having your finances on track will make you a better doctor professionally, but most importantly will lead to a happier life.

5. Cheap, simple low-cost, broadly diverse index fund should be the foundation of your portfolio and is God's gift to us investors.

6. No one can predict how the future will act (not even the online gurus), stay consistent and don't try to time the market!

7. Investing is boring and it should be; exciting investments often lead to significant losses!

8. Insure well but only against catastrophe using only cheap term life, health, professional malpractice, and disability insurance. Whole Life insurance is almost always a bad idea.

9. Live like a resident/student for 3-5 years and slowly grow into your doctor's salary. It is extremely hard for us to cut back on spending once you are used to high "doctor" spending habits.

10. Pay cash and avoid debt at all costs. Make it a goal to pay off all your student debts and all other debts. Do not leverage too much, that how a lot of people goes bankrupt. It is extremely hard for humans to borrow at a low rate and try to invest it for a higher rate. We are irrational and dumb; we will just end up spending it.

11. Maximize and utilize all tax-efficient retirement accounts; the backdoor Roth IRA is freaking awesome.

12. Get good financial advice at a fair and reasonable price. Use fee-only advisory services; otherwise learn how to invest yourself.

13. Practice Ownership is usually the quickest way for an optometrist to become a millionaire!

14. Avoid Student loan forgiveness programs. 25 years is way too long to be slave to your debt. Refinance to a lower rate, pay it off aggressively and take charge of your financial destiny!

15. When you are financially literate/free and meeting all your financial goals, do whatever make you happy even if it means buying a Tesla!

So, there you have it. *A blueprint to success.* A primer on all things finance, whether it be investing, paying off debt or insurance. Now it is your turn to go out into the world and make it happen.

Harness the knowledge you absorbed from the last two hundred pages into your personal life to achieve financial freedom and happiness. But don't let the learning stop at the end of this page.

Continue picking up books on investing and reading publications on finances. Use your knowledge to teach others. Financial freedom is the best gift you can receive. It comes through hard work and enables you to follow your passion and live a life of pure fulfillment.

About the Authors:

Dr. Dat Bui O.D (Co-Founder)

Dr. Bui is an optometrist at the Apple Wellness Center in the heart of Silicon Valley. He has a deep passion for ocular disease and healthcare technology. He started his career with $230,000 of student debt and has been focusing on strategies on attacking this massive debt such as budgeting and personal finance, along with investing. He is a big advocate for passive index funding with a small portfolio toward technology stocks.

Lastly, he wants to help all new doctors and high-earning professionals navigate toward wealth and financial independence.

Contact him: dbuiscco2015@gmail.com

Dr. Aaron Neufeld O.D (Co-Founder)

Dr. Neufeld is the owner of a 7-figure multi-doctor practice located in Los Altos, CA. A mere two years after graduation he eliminated his substantial student debt of over $150,000. He now focuses his energy on practice growth through patient-focused care, serial investing and helping others achieve financial freedom.

Dr. Neufeld believes in a balanced portfolio rooted in passive index funds, but also invests in small cap biotech stocks, private equities and real estate. Additionally, he frequently writes for industry publications and sits on advisory boards/expert panels.

Contact him: aneufeldod@gmail.com

Please feel free to connect with us:

Email: **ODsonFinance@gmail.com**

For additional resources/Articles: **www.ODsonFinance.com**

Join the Facebook conversation: **ODsonFinance Group**

Follow us on Instagram: **@ODsonFinance**

_____